KU-167-731

— T H E —
ENCYCLOPAEDIA
— O F —
SEXUAL TRIVIA

— T H E —
ENCYCLOPAEDIA
— O F —
SEXUAL TRIVIA

Dr Robin Smith

GUILD PUBLISHING

LONDON · NEW YORK · SYDNEY · TORONTO

This edition published 1990 by Guild Publishing by
arrangement with Robson Books

Copyright © 1990 Dr Robin Smith
The right of Dr Robin Smith to be identified as author
of this work has been asserted by him in accordance
with the Copyright, Designs and Patents Act 1988

CN 2606

All rights reserved. No part of this publication may
be reproduced, stored in a retrieval system, or
transmitted in any form or by any means, electronic,
mechanical, photocopying, recording or otherwise,
without the prior permission in writing of the
publishers.

Typeset and printed in Great Britain by
Butler & Tanner Ltd, Frome and London

Introduction

If you're curious to know how you measure up against the next man (or woman) but haven't liked to ask. If you remember that there was something peculiar about Ruskin's (or Swinburne's, or Hitler's or . . .) sex life but you can't remember quite what. If you're not sure what 'concrete mixing' is in Australia or what 'Six-ten' means in CB speak. If it's ever crossed your mind what the optimum speed is for a vibrator or what a 'husband's knot' really is. And if you've ever wondered where to find these and hundreds of similar answers about sex and sexuality down the ages – wonder no more. Read on.

From the oldest recorded adulterer to Frank Zappa's views on oral sex and from Attila the Hun who left this world as he came to Queen Zingua of Angola's all too literal interpretation of a one night stand – you'll find you're in good company in the pages that follow.

There are time-honoured aphrodisiacs to put you in the mood and tempting tipples to heighten your libido. You'll discover how long most lovers spend in foreplay (the tip is to make the most of it before the wedding) and who uses what to keep the family members in check. Look out for the statistics on how most people acquire a taste for sex and for how long they keep it up.

But just in case the evening doesn't go entirely according to plan, there's the comforting thought that somewhere between A and Z there will be someone who must have felt far worse off. And always remember the maxim of the American photographer, Richard Avedon, who told *Playboy* in 1975, 'He sleeps fastest who sleeps alone.'

Sweet dreams.

ADULTERER – OLDEST
In 1653 a man of eighty-nine was found guilty and executed in England for committing adultery.

ADULTERY
Adultery should be pretty cut and dried but defendants in divorce cases have offered some novel explanations for their conduct:

'I thought it meant getting a girl into trouble.'

'Adultery is having sexual intercourse with a woman not your wife, who is over fifty years of age; and it is not adultery if she is under fifty.'

'I thought it meant drinking with a man in public houses.'

'I didn't think it was adultery in the daytime.'

To the actor George Burns adultery was simply a question of

'doing to somebody else's wife what you do in the night with your own'.

Another actor, James Sanders, in court and under oath, remarked, 'It's called adultery because adults do it, but it's pretty juvenile.' Here he spoke with some authority, having been found fast asleep by a friend on the floor of his closet after the friend had come home unexpectedly while Sanders was upstairs committing adultery with his wife.

Amazons

The Amazons, those fearless female warriors of the ancient world, had a novel way of improving their 'lovers'' sexual prowess. Men taken in battle had an arm or leg broken, not to hamper their escape, but to make them more vigorous between the sheets – or so their captors fondly believed. They reckoned that if one of a captive's extremities, like an arm or a leg, was impaired, then his sex organs would be correspondingly strengthened. As Queen Antianara once proudly remarked of limping slaves, 'The lame best perform the act of love.'

Anchovies

Most seafoods have strong aphrodisiac associations, but anchovies, with their stimulating salty tang and ready accessibility, have been popular love foods for over 2,000 years, although they have taken something of a back seat this century.

The Aphrodite

The Aphrodite was an exclusive sex club that existed in eighteenth-century France until the French Revolution. Drawing its members from leading aristocrats and clergymen, its headquarters was a superb mansion, well guarded from intruders, where the two hundred or so members could disport themselves.

Some idea of the prowess they achieved can be gained from the account of a lady of noble birth who belonged to the Aphrodite for twenty years, during which time she claimed a total of 4,959 assignations. These included:

Princes and bishops	272
Monks	439
Rabbis	93
Army officers	929
Bankers	342
Musicians	119
Valets	117
Englishmen and other exiles in London during the Revolution	1,614
Uncles	2
Cousins	12

APPLES

Something about the shape of a plump, well-formed apple turned on lovers in the ancient world who used to exchange apples as love-tokens or throw them at each other as an energetic precursor to more serious foreplay.

A popular belief in medieval Germany held that an apple steeped in the perspiration of the woman you loved would get things going.

ST THOMAS AQUINAS

A regular killjoy who did much to formulate the official attitudes of the Roman Catholic Church towards sex, which he referred to as 'lust', St Thomas Aquinas asserted that only sex intended to produce children was acceptable in the eyes of the faith; everything else constituted a sin. He went as far as listing four categories of sin, in descending order of severity: bestiality;

homosexuality; any sexual position other than face to face with the woman lying on her back; and masturbation.

Aristotle

Profound as his thinking might have been on some subjects, the ancient Greek philosopher fell some way short when it came to understanding what makes human sexuality tick. 'Erection', he wrote, 'is chiefly caused by parsnips, artichokes, turnips, asparagus, candied ginger, acorns bruised to powder and drunk in muscadel, scallion sea shellfish, etc ... ' He also had it fixed in his head that a mother could manipulate her child's appearance, 'if in the act of copulation, the woman earnestly looks on the man, and fixes her mind on him, the child will resemble the father. Nay, if a woman, even in unlawful copulation, fix her mind upon her husband, the child will resemble him though he did not beget it.'

Armpitin

You don't hear anything much about Armpitin these days, but it caused a brief flurry of interest when it was reviewed in a North American pharmacological publication. Armpitin was described as being a male contraceptive which worked on the olfactory nerve and rendered men sterile for a number of days, corresponding to a number of particular molecular groups in its chemical formula. This should have been the first clue: in the paper that alerted the scientific community to Armpitin these molecular groups were written into the formula by the initials NO. Armpitin was in fact a hoax, dreamed up by a Canadian doctor named J S Greenstein.

AROUSAL — CAUSES OF FIRST SEXUAL AROUSAL IN WOMEN

1	Petting	34%
2	Psycho-sexual stimuli	32%
3	Masturbation	27%
4	Homosexual encounters	3%
5	Intercourse	2%
6	Dreaming	1%
7	Contact with animals	1%

THE ART OF KISSING

'It is ... necessary that the man be taller than the woman,' wrote the author of *The Art of Kissing* seventy years ago. 'The psychological reason for this is that he must always give the impression of being his woman's superior, both mentally and especially physically. The physical reason ... is that if he is taller than his woman, he is better able to kiss her. He must be able to sweep her into his strong arms and tower over her and look down into her eyes and cup her chin in his fingers and then bend over her face and plant his eager, virile lips on her moist, slightly parted, inviting ones. And all these are impossible when the woman is the taller of the two ... when the situation is reversed ... the physical mastery is gone, the male prerogative is gone ... nothing can be more disappointing.'

ASPARAGUS

Leaving aside its obviously phallic appearance, asparagus is rich in potassium, phosphorus and calcium which all contribute to a high energy output. Asparagus also stimulates the urinary tracts and kidneys and by association, as the seventeenth-century physician Nicholas Culpeper wrote, it 'stirreth up bodily lust in man and woman, whatever some have written to the contrary'.

Ass

According to the Roman philosopher Pliny the Elder, the right testis of an ass, worn in a bracelet, boosted sexual potency.

Attila the Hun

As the historian Edward Gibbon delicately phrased it, Attila the Hun, the terror of the Holy Roman Empire in the fifth century, 'relieved his tender anxiety' in the year 453 by taking yet another beautiful young bride to join the already sizeable collection in his harem. Historians argue whether or not Attila was a dwarf but in at least one respect his physical attributes were unimpaired. In fact on his wedding night he was applying this so enthusiastically that he burst an artery and expired on his marriage bed, suffocating in his own blood. His young consort was too petrified to summon help; his guards dared not interrupt what grew to be an impressively protracted, if uncharacteristically silent, sexual marathon and it was a good twenty-four hours before it was discovered that the 'Scourge of God' had been unexpectedly called to meet his Maker.

Beans

St Jerome forbade nuns to eat beans because he believed that they stimulated their sex organs and provoked carnal desires.

Bestseller

Naked Came the Stranger promised its author, Penelope Ashe, financial rewards on a par with many other red-blooded tales of sex in suburbia that seemed to proliferate in the 1970s. Within three days of publication sales had topped twenty thousand, the paperback rights had been negotiated and the film rights were up for grabs to the highest bidder. The story seemed as familiar as the novel's storyline – with one exception. Penelope Ashe was actually a consortium of twenty-four journalists who had got together to write a sex novel that fulfilled all of the prevailing criteria in the genre, in the hope that they could point up the absurdity of 'bestsellers' of this type.

The novel had been written in three weeks under the overall guidance of Mike McGrady, a journalist on the American paper *Newsday*. He laid down the minimum of essential guidelines with a heavy emphasis on sex; two sexual episodes were required per chapter, kinky if possible.

After the barest amount of editing, *Naked Came the Stranger* was sent to a publisher who had already made a fortune with a similar book. It was accepted eagerly.

Much of the success of the book depended on promoting the author and McGrady's sister-in-law took to the role of Penelope Ashe with ease and confidence.

'It's a dirty book?' enquired one hectoring reporter.

'It's a sexy book,' countered the author. 'Why do Americans think that sex is dirty?'

Then, in a television interview, she calmly told her audience that three-quarters of the nation's suburban families behaved like the ones in her novel.

As a spoof, *Naked Came the Stranger* was supremely successful, but to the growing anxiety of its creators it was also a runaway bestseller. Faced with burgeoning earnings they leaked the truth to the press and waited for the dust to settle.

BIBLE BLUSHING

The great American lexicographer Noah Webster, whose memory lives on in the famous dictionary that bears his name, is less well known for his attempts to clean up the Bible. Setting out his case he explained that, 'Many words and phrases are so offensive, especially to females, as to create a reluctance in young persons to attend Bible classes and schools in which they are required to read passages which cannot be repeated without a blush.'

To this end he laid into the good book in 1833, ten years before his death, replacing: 'teat' with 'breast'; 'in the belly' with 'in embryo'; 'stink' with 'smell'; 'to give suck' with 'to nurse' and 'to nourish'; 'fornication' with 'lewdness'; 'whore' with 'lewd woman' and 'prostitute'; 'to go a-whoring' with 'to go astray', and 'whoredom' with 'impurities', 'idolatries' and 'carnal connection'.

Big Breaths

The pay-off to the old joke is 'Yeth, and I'm only thixteen', though genuinely big breasts are not unknown in even younger girls. One fourteen-year-old boasted breasts weighing sixteen pounds, while a woman of thirty notched up a weight of fifty-two pounds.

In terms of length, certain African groups are endowed with extremely long, pendulous breasts more like strips of skin than the enormous bosoms of Chesty Morgan or the no less celebrated beauties displayed by Erica Rowe at Twickenham in 1982. It is not unknown for these African women to toss their breasts over their shoulders to keep them out of harm's way whilst using a pestle and mortar.

Bingo

Several years ago a fifty-five-year-old woman was awarded £10,000 damages after losing her sex drive as a result of falling off a chair while playing bingo. Her husband, whose loss it could be argued was almost as great, was awarded one two-hundredth of his wife's damages – £50.

Blindness

Does too much sex make you blind? Throughout history this message has been put about, but the fact is there *is* a grain of truth in the old myth. Syphilis is a contagious disease. Transmission is usually sexual and therefore the more sexual partners you have the greater the risk you run of contracting it.

From the very beginning syphilis affects the whole body. It manifests itself in many ways (in the past it was known as the great mimicker because its symptoms mirrored those of a good many other diseases or abnormalities). It affects the eyes in the following ways, probably contributing to the idea that too much sex does make you blind:

1 Argyll Robertson pupils − pupillary abnormalities are present in most cases of advanced syphilis and the pupils are irregular, unequal and contracted and react only slug-gishly when light is shone into them. In the later stages the pupils become much smaller and do not react at all in size as they normally should when the eyes are required to focus together on some near object.

2 Optic atrophy − here the major nerve responsible for the ability to see dies as a result of syphilis infection, and blindness results.

3 Horner's syndrome − syphilis damages the walls of the major artery from the heart (the aorta) in such a way that it balloons into a huge sack. This presses on certain involuntary nerves in the body and causes a small pupil, a retracting eyeball and a permanently closed lid on one side.

4 Reiter's syndrome − this is a rare complication of non-specific urethritis which amongst other things causes a form of conjunctivitis, with inflammation of the cornea and an abnormality of the structures at the front of the eyeball which may come and go for many years.

BODY BEAUTIFUL
According to a survey in *The Sunday Times* the ten parts of the male anatomy that British men think a woman finds irresistible are:

1 Muscular chest and shoulders   21%

2 Big biceps	18%
3 Penis	15%
4 Tall stature	13%
5 Flat stomach	9%
6 Slim figure	7%
7 Hair	4%
8 Small buttocks	4%
9 Sexy eyes	4%
10 Long legs	3%

Compare this with the list that the women in the survey produced and you can understand why so many men never get as far as even buying her the first drink. These are the parts that actually turn her on:

1 Small buttocks	39%
2 Slim figure	15%
3 Flat stomach	13%
4 Sexy eyes	11%
5 Long legs	6%
6 Tall stature	5%
7 Hair	5%
8 Neck	3%
9 Penis	2%
10 Muscular chest and shoulders	1%

NAPOLEON BONAPARTE

Somehow Napoleon's sexual conquests never matched up to his military ones. Two official marriages, at least a dozen mistresses and a good twenty casual encounters mark him down for determination if not complete success.

In Josephine he married an older woman and an insatiable libido. Josephine rarely slept alone and was infamous for her consequent affairs while Napoleon was away campaigning. As one contemporary put it, she believed that 'far sighted nature had placed the wherewithal to pay her bills beneath her navel'.

During his Egyptian campaign, Napoleon took a mistress named Pauline Fourès who was prone to dressing as a young soldier in order to spend time with her husband, a lieutenant in the army. Deviously sending him back to France, Mme Fourès spent her time with Napoleon, regularly dressing in skin-tight white pantaloons calculated to indulge his famous buttock fetish. Napoleon's chief aide-de-camp and confidant, Duroc, acted as pimp for his casual liaisons and lined up an array of luscious ladies beneath the general's sheets, who would take their turn whenever he felt the need for instant gratification.

Come 1809 and no sign of an heir from Josephine, the stormy marriage was annulled freeing the emperor to take a second wife, Marie-Louise of Austria. She was an eighteen-year-old virgin, whose upbringing had been so sheltered that even male animals had been removed from her presence lest they corrupt her. Napoleon plainly saw more in her than youth alone and, anxious for an heir, stated baldly that she had 'the kind of womb I want to marry'.

By the time he was forty-two, however, the emperor was impotent, confirming Josephine's sour comment that 'bon-a-part est bon à rien'.

On his death it was discovered that he had fairly full feminine breasts and that his penis had shrunk to barely an inch in length. For reasons not fully understood this was preserved for some 150 years, when it came to auction but failed to reach the reserve, perhaps because of the unappealing catalogue entry which described it as 'a small dried-up object'. It finally ended up in the hands of an American urologist who offered £2,500 for this little piece of history.

JAMES BOSWELL

Dr Johnson's friend and biographer, James Boswell, was also an enthusiastic follower of the ladies, with no false modesty about his powers or his passion. Two of his favourite boasts were his ability to make love five times in a row and to have contracted gonorrhoea seventeen times!

BREACH OF THE PEACE

When police in New York City arrested a naked twenty-seven-year-old model, a photographer and a freelance journalist on a street corner in Manhattan – in broad daylight – they assumed they had an open-and-shut case. In court the judge found otherwise.

The fact that the young lady had been standing on the junction of Broadway with Liberty Street as naked as the day she was born while she was photographed did not apparently constitute sufficient grounds for a conviction on the charge before the court.

As the judge said, 'Actually the defendants annoyed no one, interfered with no one, obstructed no one, except perhaps the police officers. A breach of the peace requires the presence of the public.' The public related to people. There weren't any people there. So he dismissed the charge and acquitted the three of them.

BREATH CONTROL

In the year 138, the Greek physician Soranus offered this apparently flawless method of contraception: 'The woman ought, in the moment during coitus when the man ejaculates his sperm, to hold her breath, draw her body back a little so that the semen cannot penetrate the Os Uteri, then immediately get up and sit down with bent knees and, in this position, provoke sneezes.'

BREWING

At one time brewers would refuse to have sex while the fermentation of their best beers reached its own climax.

CAD

Several years ago Geoffrey Smith ran a competition in *The Sunday Times* to find the best definition of a cad. From this he learned (and shared the intelligence with his readers) that the cad is the man 'who forgets that gentlemen always use their elbows'. He's also the one to give the girl a baby and then blame her for not taking the pill. His other failings in this area include keeping his sterility a secret until his wife announces happily that she is pregnant. He'll also enjoy a lady's favours and then broadcast the fact to the world by returning her knickers in a transparent envelope — by post. Catherine Hunt, one of the correspondents to reply to Geoffrey Smith's enquiry, offered a string of caddish attributes: 'he does your crossword when you're out; votes SDP; eats all the peanuts you were saving for Friday night; shows his friends your letters; tells you whodunit; calls breasts "Bristols"; and is the one you want to go out with more than anyone in the world.'

CALORIE COUNT

The average man's ejaculate packs just five calories, although it is rich in protein. So one thing oral sex *won't* do is make you fat.

CANDID CAMERA

'Sex kitten seeks sharp cat! Send candid pictures', ran the advertisement placed in a local contacts magazine by Ilsa Schmidt, tiring of her husband but frisky enough to look for kicks elsewhere. Klaus Schmidt evidently shared his wife's feelings — his was one of the enthusiastic replies she received. Once Frau Schmidt had recovered her composure she filed for divorce, stating that this was the first time she had ever seen her husband naked. Whenever they made love he always insisted on doing it in the dark.

CARAWAY

Caraway is traditionally a popular ingredient of love potions. For centuries it has also been recommended to ease digestion. As such it was frequently offered in the form of sweets and similar confections at the end of banquets and after excessive feasting to help the diners regain some internal comfort before retiring to enjoy the delights of bed as well as board.

CASANOVA

Casanova has become a synonym for any great lover or seducer. The original article was tall, dark, well-built and was intelligent and witty into the bargain. At various times he was a writer, gambler and traveller. He also dabbled in the occult and took a turn in practising homoeopathy at one stage in his life. He was imprisoned for sexual offences, he had a duel over a woman with a Polish count, and was reputed to have had venereal disease on at least eleven occasions.

When it came to seduction Casanova was a great believer in perseverance, maintaining that 'there is not a woman in the world who could resist constant attentions'. He spent most of his life putting his theory into practice. His success can be judged by his twelve-volume *Histoire de Ma Vie* which was partly written during his sojourn in prison. Many of his claims made in this were borne out by various witnesses, and Casanova's tally of 150 women whose favours he enjoyed may well be on the conservative side.

After losing his virginity at eleven he continued to be sexually active until the age of fifty. Of the women that fell under his spell, twenty-four were servants, eighteen came from the aristocracy, fifteen had royal blood, and two were nuns. He also counted a dozen or more prostitutes and one slave among his conquests. Other statistics show that he deflowered thirty-one virgins, seduced his partners thirty-one times, was seduced by them on a dozen occasions, made love to them by mutual attraction on thirty-six occasions and was rejected no fewer than sixteen times.

Casanova was an early pioneer of the contraceptive sheath although he had reservations about the way it blunted sensitivity and often referred to the sheath as the 'English overcoat'; his experiments with half a lemon are referred to elsewhere (see Dutch Caps).

Six years after commencing his well documented career, the seventeen-year-old Casanova indulged in his first ménage à trois with a couple of sisters whom he apparently coaxed into a false sense of security by feigning sleep in their bed. After winning over first one sister and then the other, and enjoying a mutual washing, the three aroused themselves into such a frenzy that they spent the rest of the night 'in ever varying skirmishes'. His sexual tastes were not restricted to women, however, and on another occasion at a convent in Mirano, Casanova freely indulged in another intimate threesome with a beautiful young nun (with a very catholic sex drive) and her lover. Casanova, as usual, successfully got in on the act and 'intoxicated by desire, and transported by continual furies, played havoc with everything visible and palpable, freely devouring whatever we saw and finding that we had all become of the same sex in all the trios we performed'.

During his lifetime he also indulged in a little incest and once said, 'I have never been able to understand how a father could tenderly love his charming daughter without having slept with her at least once'. Before the age of forty, however, his sexual activities began to flag. By 1763 he was actually advertising in London for companions, and he resorted to revisiting old flames in Europe as well as taking up the opportunities presented by encounters with prostitutes. Casanova was probably celibate during his thirteen years as a librarian in Bohemia, and finally became totally impotent towards the end of his life.

CHINESE TAKE-AWAYS
In an effort to help curb the nation's growing population a pharmacy in the Chinese city of Tientsin began distributing contraceptives free of charge. However, it soon became obvious that many people were too embarrassed to ask for them, possibly because of the four sizes in which they were offered: large, medium, small and extra small (or miniature). To get round the problem it was decided to open a self-service take-away instead.

CHOCOLATE
In seventeenth-century France monks were forbidden to drink chocolate on account of its reputed aphrodisiac properties. A century later chocolate cropped up in a large number of aphrodisiac recipes.

CIRCUMCISION

Circumcision has been viewed by many British authorities as rather archaic. Forty years ago Sir James Spence said as much in a letter to a colleague, 'If you can show good reason why a ritual designed to ease the penalties of concupiscence amongst the sand and flies of the Syrian deserts should be continued in this England of clean bed linen and lesser opportunity, I shall listen to your argument; but if you base your argument upon anatomical faults, then I must refute it. The anatomists have never studied the form and evolution of the preputial orifice. They do not understand that Nature does not intend it to be stretched and retracted in the Temples of the Welfare Centres, or ritually removed ... '

CLITORIS

The average clitoris is one inch long, though it must be remembered that for most, if not all of its length it is hooded, that is covered by a flap of tissue at the top of the vulva. The prevailing indifference in the nineteenth century, and at the beginning of the present one, towards sexual arousal in women largely neglected the importance of the clitoris. But, however small, it is always liberally endowed with sensitive nerve endings which make it, in the words of one sexologist, 'a veritable electrical bell button which, when pressed, will ring up the whole nervous system'.

COCK

The 1933 edition of the *Oxford English Dictionary* explains that 'cock' '... is the current name among the people, but, *pudoris causa*, not admissible in polite speech or literature'. Its origin is connected with the medieval meaning of cock which was, 'a spout or short pipe serving as a channel for passing liquids through, and having an appliance for regulating or stopping the flow'.

Until this century it did not make many appearances in respectable literature (though *Henry V* includes the line 'Pistol's cock is up' – which means what it says) and the word was never spoken in polite society – even when it referred to the male hen rather than the male member. A barnyard cock became a rooster and a 'cock-and-bull tale' featuring three hapless words open to misinterpretation, was transformed to a 'rooster and ox story'. People with cock in their names have long felt sensitive and often prefer you to forget the 'ck' at the end, so pronouncing Cockburn as Co'burn and Hiscock as Hisco.

The fact that the word 'cock' has so many connotations is one of its charms and allows the less-than-innocent much harmless amusement.

COCKSURE

Not long ago one of the racier British newspapers was introducing readers to 'studs with massive manhoods', highlighting the latest in a proud tradition of naughty nicknames of which these are fifty firm favourites:

Laughing Carrot	Percy	Bone
Meat Whistle	Chopper	Dong
Lung Disturber	John Thomas	Private
Pyjama Python	Beard Splitter	Pink Oboe
Porridge Pump	Organ	Gadget
Kidney Wiper	Beef Bayonet	Mutton Dagger
Pork	Dork	Ice Cream Maker
Brigadier	Schwanz	Willy Banana
Ferret	Trouser Snake	Bent Stick
Phallus Organ	Club	Wife's Best Friend
Gun	Pecker	Bald Headed
Pole	Dave	Hermit

Candy Bar	Thing	Rod
Tool	Widget	Penny Whistle
Matrimonial Peace-maker	Dick	Charlie
	Willy	Wanger
Bacon Roll	Prick	Knob
Jock		

COD PIECES
Seeking ever-inventive ways of packaging and marketing their fish products, Bird's Eye hit on a tasty morsel in 1976 – Cod Pieces. Product development was surprisingly far advanced before the penny dropped.

CONFESSION
In 1714 the Roman Catholic Church decreed that men confessing to fornication need no longer name the partners with whom they had sinned because too many priests were making improper use of the information.

CONTRABAND
Before the death of General Franco in 1975 and the subsequent loosening of social and moral taboos in Spain, contraceptives smuggled in from North Africa formed a lucrative and busy side of the trade in contraband. Dogs saddled with pouches were used to carry the precious commodities from the beaches up into the hills from whence their owners could distribute them as the market demanded.

Contraceptive Success

Contraceptives may not work for a number of reasons: couples may forget to use them altogether; they may use them incorrectly; and the chosen method may malfunction. A study made twenty-five years ago showed that the likelihood of pregnancy occurring among one hundred couples using each of the methods below was:

Contraceptive Method	Pregnancy Rate
Douche	31 out of 100
Rhythm	24 out of 100
Spermicide jelly	20 out of 100
Withdrawal	18 out of 100
Condom	14 out of 100
Diaphragm	12 out of 100
Spermicide foam	8–12 out of 100
IUD	5 out of 100
Sequential pill	5 out of 100
Combination pill	0.1 out of 100
Vasectomy	Practically 0

Corkscrew Penis

This is a puzzling condition that sometimes affects bulls. Instead of achieving a conventional erection prior to mating, sufferers of this disorder are thwarted by the distortion of their penises which spring into a corkscrew shape, making penetration of the cow virtually impossible.

Coughs and Sneezes

Sexual Physiology, written by Dr Russell Thacker Thrall in the middle of the last century, cast an unusual and to many no doubt hopeful light on the nature of contraception. The author maintained that during travels in the Friendly Isles and Iceland he had come across 'some women [who] have that flexibility and vigour of the whole muscular system that they can, by effort of will, prevent conception'. He also informed his readers that 'sometimes coughing or sneezing will have the same effect. Running, jumping, lifting and dancing are often resorted to successfully'.

Perhaps the aerobics boom of the 1980s has an explanation after all.

CUCUMBERS
Thirty reasons why cucumbers are better than men:

1 The average cucumber is at least six inches longer.
2 Cucumbers stay hard for two weeks.
3 A cucumber won't tell you that size doesn't matter.
4 Cucumbers don't get too excited.
5 Cucumbers are easy to pick up.
6 You can fondle cucumbers in a supermarket and see how firm they are before you take one home.
7 A cucumber will always respect you in the morning.
8 You can go to a film with a cucumber and see the film.
9 A cucumber won't ask 'Am I the first?'
10 A cucumber won't tell other cucumbers that you aren't a virgin any more.
11 With cucumbers you don't have to be a virgin more than once.
12 Cucumbers won't make you wear kinky clothes or go to bed with your boots on.
13 You can have as many cucumbers as you can handle.
14 You only eat cucumbers when you feel like it.
15 Cucumbers are not into meaningful discussions.
16 Cucumbers are not jealous of your gynaecologist, ski instructor or hairdresser.

17 Cucumbers will never make a scene because there are other cucumbers in the fridge.

18 No matter how old you are you can always get a fresh cucumber.

19 A cucumber won't mind what time of the month it is.

20 With a cucumber you never have to say you're sorry.

21 Cucumbers won't leave you wondering for a month.

22 Cucumbers do not leave carpet burns, fall asleep on your chest or drool on the pillow.

23 Cucumbers never answer your phone or borrow your car.

24 Cucumbers can stay all night without you having to sleep on the wet spot.

25 A cucumber will never leave you for another woman, another man or another cucumber.

26 You won't find out later that your cucumber is married, is on penicillin, or liked you but loved your brother.

27 You don't have to wait until half-time to talk to your cucumber.

28 A cucumber will not expect you to have little cucumbers.

29 Cucumbers do not worry about more skilful courgettes.

30 You can have your cucumber – and eat it.

CUNT

'Cunt' is as explicit and as universal as 'cock', but it is a shade more shocking and not nearly so versatile. Of all the words used to describe the female genitalia 'cunt' is the oldest. Robert Burchfield, in his magisterial Supplement to the *Oxford English Dictionary*, provides ten literary references for the word, covering 750 years, from 'Gropecuntlane' around 1230 to a line from Samuel Beckett's *Malone Dies* in 1956, 'His young wife had abandoned all hope of bringing him to heel by means of her cunt, that trump card of young wives.' Those that resent the harshness of the word 'cunt' will regret that 'cunny', popular in the eighteenth and nineteenth centuries, is no longer in regular use.

'Cunt' has given us other words. If you are 'cunt-struck' you are a man who enjoys cunts; if you have a 'cunt-itch' or 'cunt-stand' you are a woman in need of satisfaction; if you are a 'cunt-pensioner' you are a pimp, and if you've a can of 'Sprunt' you have found a vaginal deodorant. (The name Sprunt was devised by one of the world's largest deodorant manufacturers when they were developing their 'cunt spray' in the late 1960s.)

Cup Size

The average female bust measurement is between thirty-five and thirty-six inches, though bra manufacturers have reported a modest increase in bust size over the last decade or two, which they attribute to better nutrition and more widespread use of the pill.

CLEMENCE DANE

The novelist and playwright Clemence Dane (Winifred Ashton was her real name) was celebrated for the matchless bloomers she delivered with apparent innocence and (for her friends) alarming ease. Here are six of the best:

To the actress Joyce Carey in the crowded foyer of the Old Vic: 'But Joyce, it's well known that Shakespeare sucked Bacon dry.'

In answer to an enquiry about some goldfish last seen in a pool in the blazing sun: 'Oh, they're all right now. They've got a vast erection covered with everlasting pea.'

To dinner guests one evening: 'We're having roast cock tonight.'

In a ghost story she wrote: 'Night after night for weeks she tried to make him come ...'

A sculptor herself, she gave classes to her friends and once corrected Noël Coward's technique with the words: 'Noël, dear boy, you must wipe your tool. You cannot work with a dirty tool.'

On another occasion she demonstrated how the clay should be worked on the armature: 'Now then, stick it right up, ram it, ram it, ram it and work away, either from the back or front, whichever comes easiest! Some people use a lubricant. I've used honey in my time! And remember, when you've finished you must withdraw it wiggle, waggle, wiggle, waggle, very gently.'

DAVID
The personal column of *The Times* once carried the following advertisement, 'Statue required, size approximately four-feet-seven-inches to five feet, reproduction of Michelangelo's *David*, without fig leaf.'

DEAFNESS
Just as exposure to syphilis causes eye problems, so can it affect the eighth cranial (auditory) nerve and cause a degree of deafness.

DEVIL
The first woman reported to have been burned at stake for having sex with the devil was a citizen of Toulouse, who met her fate in 1275 after apparently giving birth to a child with the head of a wolf and a tail like a snake.

DILDOS
At one time it was common for French soldiers to leave their wives with dildos (artificial penises) when they marched off to war, to reduce the risk of adultery while they were away.

Dirty Dog

Franco Boretti, a proud pet-owner from Sicily, was taken to court and given two fines amounting to the equivalent of 67p each after his dog had been found guilty of committing 'an obscene act in a public place'.

Outside the court room he told waiting reporters, 'I resent Blackie being branded a playdog by the gutter press.

'It is quite true that he had the pharmacist's poodle bitch twice in fifteen minutes on the steps of the Convent of St Mary, but he has had almost every bitch in Porto Venus over the past three years. I don't see what is so special about a mangy poodle.'

Acknowledging that his friendship with the owner of the ravaged poodle had ended, Signor Boretti said, 'We had played dominoes together for close on sixty years. What does he expect me to do? Show Blackie the two fine tickets? As for having my animals fixed – I would rather go to Russia'.

DIY

Ten popular euphemisms for masturbation:

Beat the Meat	Five Finger Knuckle Shuffle
Shake the Snake	Bang the Bishop
Hand Job	J Arthur
Lesbian Frank	Syphon the Python
Gallop the Maggot	Flog the Donkey

Dreams

In most cases men have erections when they dream – even those who have had sex before falling asleep. However, anxious dreams produce smaller erections than those that bring more pleasurable fantasies.

DRESSING

According to studies into the side on which men 'dress', seventy-five per cent have penises that lie to the left when they're fully clothed as opposed to a mere seventeen per cent that have penises that lie to the right. The remainder seem able to lie on one side or the other.

DUNES

Making love alfresco in the sand dunes is graphically termed 'concrete mixing' in Australia.

DUNG

During the reign of the pharaohs a popular contraceptive for Egyptian women was a pessary made of elephant and crocodile dung.

DUTCH CAP

One of the most imaginative Dutch caps ever invented and put to practical use was the half lemon that Casanova habitually carried with him. In addition to this he favoured a condom made from a sheep's intestine and a collection of two-ounce gold balls which seemingly brought security and immense satisfaction to his partners.

EARLY SEXUAL POSITIONS
Ancient art from the early civilizations of South America, India and China shows many instances of couples having sex with the woman on top of her partner. This evidence is backed up by early cave paintings in Europe too. Other positions depicted show rear entry and sex with both partners standing up.

EARS
In the history of sex the otherwise innocent ear has had a pretty bad deal. In the Middle Ages it was generally accepted that women's ears turned men on to the same extent as the more obvious feminine attributes; that is why so many medieval headdresses ensured that women's ears were discreetly covered. Even after the Renaissance and the rebirth of learning had reached these shores ears were still having a rough ride. Henry VIII's doctors, for instance, were convinced that the King's venereal disease was due to Cardinal Wolsey recklessly whispering in one of the Royal ears.

ELECTION FEVER
The Pigalle restaurant celebrated a general election thirty years ago by dressing a line of chorus girls exclusively in blue, red and yellow rosettes. Every time a seat was lost by one of the three leading political parties off would come a rosette: blue for the Tories, red for Labour and yellow for the Liberals, as they then were.

ERECTION
Can you tell how big a penis will be when it is erect by looking at it when it's limp?

No — and this is why.

The man who is convinced that his little clam-digger is much smaller than that of his peers will be delighted to discover that he is much more likely to have a greater co-efficient of linear expansion than his mates. In other words, small flaccid penises tend to expand to a much greater degree than penises that are already quite large when resting, so that both will reach the average erect size of six inches or so.

An erection is caused by blood being pumped into the penis in response to sexual arousal. Just as an uninflated balloon gives little idea of its potential size and shape when inflated, so a limp penis gives just as poor an idea of its size when erect. Thickness and elasticity of the skin, the area of sponge-like tissue within, and the volume of blood being pumped into the organ will determine its erect dimensions.

EROGENOUS ZONES
Erogenous zones, the ones that respond quickest to sexual stimulation, are dotted all over the female form and in some of the most unlikely places. The list below gives fifteen of the commonest, though some achieve more dramatic results than others. From head to toe they are:

1 Ears
2 Eyelids
3 Mouth
4 Tongue
5 Neck
6 Nipples
7 Underarms
8 Palms of hands
9 Fingertips
10 Buttocks
11 Anus
12 Vaginal labia
13 Clitoris
14 Inner thighs
15 Toes

EROTICA

Among the results of his wide-ranging research into human sexuality Alfred Kinsey discovered what does and does not arouse both men and women:

Men who get stimulated by erotic photographs	77%
Women who get stimulated by erotic photographs	32%
Men who get stimulated by sexy literature	59%
Women who get stimulated by sexy literature	60%
Men who get stimulated by hearing dirty stories	47%
Women who get stimulated by hearing dirty stories	14%

EROTIC CIRCUS

Among the shadier entertainments in the Paris of the 1930s was the *cirque érotique*, or 'erotic circus' which combined all the fun of the race meeting with the raciest of nightclub shows. Naked women cycled energetically round an indoor track as spectators placed bets on which of them would reach orgasm first from the rubbing of clitoris on saddle.

ETIQUETTE
According to a manual of etiquette published in the 1840s, readers were advised that, 'Care should be taken not to place books by authors of different sexes next to each other'.

EUNUCHS
Surprising as it sounds, it is possible to have sex without testicles; it may not be quite as much fun, but it is possible all the same, under certain circumstances. Providing that the castration is restricted to cutting off the testicles alone (sometimes the whole kit would go), it is possible for a man's libido and ability to indulge in intercourse not to be reduced at all. Oriental history abounds with tales of randy eunuchs who enjoyed many a romp in the harem while the sultan's back was turned.

EXCITEMENT — FEMALE
Six areas for sexually exciting women in order of precedence:

1 Clitoris
2 Vagina near clitoris
3 Inside lips of vulva
4 Inside vagina
5 Breasts
6 Outside lips of vulva

EXETER RIDDLE

Included in the Old English poems collected in the *Exeter Book* towards the end of the tenth century is the riddle which, in translation, runs:

> A strange thing hangs by a man's thigh, under its master's clothes. It is pierced at the front, is stiff and hard, has a good fixed place. When the man lifts his clothes up above the knee, he wishes then to place the head of the hanging object into the familiar hole which it, when of equal length, has often filled before.

Any ideas?

The answer, of course, is a key.

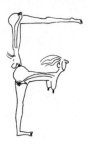

FART

Technically 'an anal escape of wind, especially if audible', the fart has a literary pedigree stretching right back to Chaucer. Its uses are various (a 'fart-catcher' is a footman who walks behind; a 'fart-sucker' is a parasite; 'like a fart in a bottle' indicates flustered agitation; 'don't fart about' means stop fooling; and 'a silly fart' is a contemptuous description of a silly fool), but it is still in its original and anatomical sense that we use the word most frequently.

John Aubrey, in his outrageous *Brief Lives*, tells the glorious story of a fart in high places. It concerns Elizabeth I and one of her courtiers, Edward de Vere, seventeenth Earl of Oxford:

> This Earl of Oxford, making of his low obeisance to Queen Elizabeth, happened to let a Fart, at which he was so abashed and ashamed that he went to Travell, 7 yeares. On his return the Queen welcomed him home, and said, 'My Lord, I had forgott the Fart.'

Fast Cars

Ten reasons why fast cars are better than fast women:

1 Fast expensive cars only whine when something is really wrong.
2 Fast cars don't pull away from you if you handle them badly.
3 Fast cars don't complain if you're late.
4 Fast cars don't mind if you buy fast car magazines.
5 If the seat sags in your fast car it doesn't cost the earth to refurbish it.
6 Fast cars always want to go for a ride.
7 Your parents won't keep in touch with your old fast car after you've dumped it and got a newer model.
8 Fast cars don't complain if you hold tighter as the pace hots up.
9 Your pals will usually let you try out their new fast cars.
10 Fast cars are always well lubricated.

Felix Faure

In the last year of the nineteenth century the French president, Félix Faure was enjoying his mistress's favours in a specially designed sex chair when he had a heart attack and died on the job.

Feminine Hygiene

The makers of sanitary towels have promoted their wares in a number of ingenious ways over the years, but few have shown the same initiative as that of Southall Brothers and Barclay of Birmingham who, in July 1888, took up one third of the back cover of *The Antiquary* with an advertisement. This was particularly addressed to 'Ladies travelling by Land and Sea'. The commodities themselves were referred to as 'patented Articles of Underclothing. Indispensable to ladies Travelling. Sold at

Cost of Washing Only! To burn when done with. Of Drapers and Ladies' Outfitters Everywhere.'

First Night Rights
It was the Scottish King Ewen III who dreamt up the idea of the right of the first night, around the year 875. A chronicle that recorded his reign incudes this fascinating footnote to history, 'Another law that he made, that wives of common men shall be free to the nobles; and the Lord of the ground shall have the maidenheads of all the virgins dwelling in the same'. King Ewen's brainwave remained a popular pastime until the beginning of the Middle Ages.

First Sex
The word 'sex' made its first appearance in English in 1382 when John Wyclif used it in his translation of the Old Testament (*Genesis* VI. 19): 'Of alle thingis havynge sowle of only flesh, two thow shalt brynge into the ark, that maal sex and femaal lyven with thee.'

First Time Lucky
Attitudes towards first sexual experiences differ. One survey produced statistics such as:

1 Women who were 'in love' with the first man
   they slept with   50%
2 Men who were 'in love' with the first woman
   they slept with   10%
3 Men who were 'happy' after their first taste
   of sexual intercourse   90%
4 Women who were 'happy' after the first time   66%
5 Women who did not tell anybody else about

their first sexual experience 25%
6 Men who did not tell anybody else about it 18%
7 Women who told more than five people 22%
8 Men who told more than five people 63%

FLAGELLANT

Flagellant was the school magazine compiled by the poet Robert Southey while he was a pupil at Westminster. It has the unique distinction among school magazines of being confined to the closed case of the British Library.

FLASHERS

According to the sex researcher, Havelock Ellis, ' ... as early as 1476 a London priest appeared before the Ecclesiastical Court charged with showing his privates to several women in the parish ... No doubt his sacred profession led to the scandal. We are not told that anything was done about it.'

FLAT CHESTS

Mongolian women are reckoned to have the world's flattest female chests in a society where mammaries are considered appalling deformities. In Western society where the reverse is manifestly the case, the earliest recorded surgical breast reduction didn't take place until 1731.

ERROL FLYNN

Errol Flynn, the swashbuckling hero of Hollywood adventures in the 1930s and 1940s, started life as a natural tearaway, leaving home at an early age to become a sailor cruising the southern oceans in a variety of employments. It was during one of these that he was spotted by a talent scout and signed up by Warner Brothers.

His muscular build, boyish charm and natural sense of fun and adventure made him a popular screen idol with men and women alike. Errol Flynn claimed to have spent at least 13,000 nights in the arms of one women or another and although he was married three times, he spent most of his time away from his wives and children. 'The only real wives I have ever had are my sailing ships', he is reputed to have once said.

He enjoyed oriental sex techniques, picked up during his days in the Far East, and was keen on applying a pinch of cocaine to the tip of his penis to act as an aphrodisiac. He liked voyeurism too and once installed a two-way mirror in his home to spy on guests as they made love. He also suffered from a morbid fear of castration which lingered with him throughout his life; possessed of plenty, as he saw it, he realized how much he had to lose.

On two separate but very well publicized occasions Errol Flynn was accused of statutory rape. Acquittals on both occasions added to his screen reputation as a charming rogue and the phrase 'in like Flynn' became popular among servicemen boasting of the pleasure they had had and given in their latest sexual conquests.

FOREPLAY
Foreplay tails off after marriage – that's the simple message. Whereas pre-marital foreplay averages thirty-two minutes, foreplay between married partners lasts only just over half as long at a rather hasty seventeen minutes. Only one in twenty married men sustain foreplay for half-an-hour or longer.

Fuck

As Edward Sagarin noted so eloquently in *The Anatomy of Dirty Words*:

> In the entire language of proscribed words, from slang to profanity, from the mildly unclean to the utterly obscene, including terms relating to concealed parts of the body, to excretion and excrement as well as to sexuality, one word reigns supreme, unchallenged in its pre-eminence. It sits upon a throne, an absolute monarch, unafraid of any princely off-spring still unborn and by its subjects it is hated, feared, revered and loved, known by all and recognized by none.

Frankly, 'fuck' is a better word for sexual intercourse than any other. It is unambiguous and to the point. The rest are highly unsatisfactory: 'to sleep with' is the reverse of the truth; 'to make love' is far from always the case; 'to screw' implies male conquest and female submission in altogether too sexist a way; 'to copulate' is technical; 'to fornicate' is legalistic; 'to bang' is too loud; 'to bunk up' sounds uncomfortable; and 'to get it on', 'to have it away', and 'to have it in', are three very crude euphemisms.

'Fuck' has been around for at least 500 years (it was listed synonymously with 'sard', 'swive' and 'occupy' in John Florio's *Worlde of Words* in 1598), but the Supplement to the *Oxford English Dictionary* protests that its etymology is unknown. It may be related to the German *ficken* (to strike) and the Latin *pungere* (to prick), but the connections have not been proven. There are still some people who believe that the word began as an acronym: in the Middle Ages, when a couple were convicted of fornication, the bailiff would enter in his book – 'For unlawful carnal knowledge', which, as business as brisk and prosecutions plenty, was usually abbreviated to F.u.c.k. It's a charming story, but true.

Whatever its origins, 'fuck's' meaning is now universally recognized. As a noun it can represent the act of intercourse ('Do you want a fuck?) and a person viewed in terms of intercourse ('He's a fantastic fuck!'). As a verb it means simply 'to copulate' and the Supplement to the *Oxford English Dictionary* traces its literary use as a verb as far back as 1503, when the poet (and sometime Franciscan friar) William Dunbar included this line in one of his verses: 'Be his feiris he wald have fukkit'.

Of the fourteen other literary references given to the verb in the *Dictionary*, three seem particularly tantalizing. Each line speaks volumes about the lives of the real people (in the first two instances) and the characters (in the third example) involved, and if ever you feel in need of a cure for insomnia just memorize one of these quotations, take it to bed with you, and try to imagine the events that could have preceded and followed the moment described in each of the brief extracts. The first comes from one of the letters of Dante Gabriel Rossetti, dated 15 September 1869, 'If Byron f——d his sister he f——d and there an end'.

The next dates from 1888–94 and comes from that lecher's *vade mecum*, *My Secret Life* by Frank Harris, 'Then a dread came over me. I had fucked a common street nymph.'

The most recent is from a translation of *Between Blue and Blue*, a French novel by Raymond Queneau, best known for *Zazie in the Metro*, ' "Well, Lamelie", said Cidrolin, "while you're waiting to get married, do you want to be entertained or educated?"

' "No, Dad, what I want to do is to fuck." '

Famous writer and critic Marghanita Laski expressed her amazement at the strange treatment given to 'such words as those till recently written as f-dash and c-dash'.

She confronted her radio listeners with two words on facing pages of the *Oxford English Dictionary*'s Supplement. The two words, in alphabetical order, 'gamahuche' and 'gamatangium'.

The first of the two should send shivers of disgust up your

spine. While 'gamatangium' has to do with cell-formation, to 'gamahuche' is to practise fellatio or cunnilingus.

GAMES PEOPLE PLAY

There must be something about sporting events that brings out the unexpected in live radio and television commentaries. Six examples for recent years show what can go so innocently wrong:

1 Discussing the seeding of players in the men's singles at Wimbledon one year, Peter West remarked of one of the hopefuls, 'Jimmy Connors's wife is expecting a baby and there was some doubt about his entry.'

2 At another tennis tournament, the Braniff Airways men's doubles tournament, Dan Maskell allowed patriotism to run away with him when David Lloyd and Mark Cox put up what might best be termed a 'spunky' performance, 'The British boys are now adopting the attacking position – Cox up.'

3 At the 1976 Montreal Olympics one television commentator was moved to oratorical heights by the exploits of the Cuban middle distance runner and 800 metre gold medallist, Alberto Juantorena. As one of his

thrilling races reached its climax, viewers were told, 'And now Juantorena opens wide his legs and shows his class.'

4 Brian Johnston stands supreme among cricket commentators for his prowess with *double entendre*. In 1976 he told listeners to the West Indies Test at the start of a new over, 'The bowler's Holding, the batsman's Willey.'

5 Down in Australia Brian Johnston cast a knowing eye round the field and told his audience of millions that Neil Harvey was standing with his legs apart, waiting for a tickle.

6 Best of all, perhaps, was his splendid spoonerism that came from an ambitious attempt to say of one player, 'He's sticking out his bottom – like someone sitting on a shooting stick.'

Greta Garbo

During the shooting of the 1935 film *Anna Karenina*, Greta Garbo took such a violent dislike to her co-star, Fredric March, that she used to munch garlic before filming their love scenes. Thirty-four years later, Diana Rigg used garlic to curtail her love scenes with George Lazenby when he took over as James Bond for his only screen appearance as 007 in *On Her Majesty's Secret Service* in 1969.

Garlic

Garlic is one of the most widely used aphrodisiacs around the world, with a pedigree that stretches back to ancient times. Its popularity in Mediterranean food may have something to do with the reputation of the Latin Lover. What's more, some scientific research suggests that the main component of garlic's volatile oil is the same essential organic chemical as the hormone secreted by women when they are sexually aroused.

GENTLE TOUCH

Several years ago *Chatelaine Magazine* carried this piece of advice:

> The solution for male doctors who do rough pelvic exams on women might begin in medical schools, where each male student would be placed in stirrups and a strange female MD would come and 'squeeze his balls and leave without saying a word'.

(This was the idea of a female gynaecologist, writing in the *Annals of Internal Medicine*.)

GETTING YOU GOING

An American report into male sexuality revealed that the following proportions of men found these stimuli 'exciting':

1 A woman taking the initiative	80%
2 Perfume and other fragrances	77%
3 Lacy lingerie	75%
4 A woman using sexually explicit language	45%
5 Vaginal odour	40%

GINSENG

The Chinese have known ginseng as 'the elixir of life' for more than 5,000 years. It forms part of the diet of Soviet space crews and its biological name in Latin means 'all healing'. Nutrition experts argue over the various merits of ginseng, but its proponents point to its three main powers: slowing down the ageing process; giving stamina and endurance, and acting as an aphrodisiac.

Goat Glands

According to bogus sexologist Dr John R Brinkley, goat glands held the secret to combating male impotence and over a period of twenty years he amassed a fortune of more than $12 million administering them to 16,000 men worried about their sexual inadequacies. But goat glands were by no means his only forte. Backed by a string of dud degrees he started his therapeutic career with a newspaper advertisement in Greenville, South Carolina which posed the question, 'Are You a Manly Man Full of Vigour?' To those who answered with a truthful 'no', the good doctor could offer an injection of distilled water (coloured) for a snip at just twenty-five dollars.

Goat's Eyelid

From the thirteenth century, when it was introduced into the court during the Yuan dynasty in China, the goat's eyelid, or happy ring, became a popular sex aid. The device was exactly what its name suggests. Following the killing of a goat, the animal's eyelids were removed, complete with the eyelashes. After being placed in quicklime to dry, they were steamed for twelve hours — a process that was repeated several times. Transferred from goat to human being, the eyelid could be tied to an erect penis before intercourse in order to provide the woman with a stimulating tickling sensation.

GOING FOR BUST

Small is not only beautiful, it's also much safer — that at least was the message in a magazine for in-flight attendants which carried a report warning air stewardesses of the potential hazards of certain silicone breast implants. Scientists had discovered that a sudden drop in cabin pressure had caused some types of implants to swell rapidly. This presumably posed a risk to airline uniforms; was likely to distract passengers (the male ones at any rate) at a time when they should have been paying attention to the cabin staff for rather different reasons; and carried the ultimate danger of the implant exploding.

GOOD VIBRATIONS

The forerunner of the 'mile-high club', for those who have coupled in an aircraft in flight, was the nineteenth-century fraternity who made it in a railway carriage. This pastime attracted such an enthusiastic following that several of the better equipped European brothels provided chambers decorated like railway carriages which shuddered and vibrated mechanically when they were occupied, as well as resounding with chugging and whistling sound effects.

GRAFFITI

When Alfred Kinsey and his team went into the closet to examine graffiti in male and female lavatories they found that men wrote and drew more sexual graffiti than women. Four out of five graffiti in male lavatories had a sexual theme, while on the other side of the wall only one in four of those created by women dealt with overt sexual subjects; love and romance seemed to be their principal occupation.

GRAHAM CRACKERS

As well as inventing the thin crisp biscuit that bears his name, Sylvester Graham was also the author of one of the most amusing condemnations of sex ever to see the light of day. Under the catchy title 'A Lecture to Young Men on Chastity, Intended Also for the Serious Consideration of Parents and Guardians, he included among his many warnings that 'highly seasoned food, rich dishes, and free use of flesh' led to almost certain insanity. He also offered dire predictions to couples (Graham couldn't even consider the possibility they might not be married) that going at it like knives would lead to 'languor, lassitude, muscular relaxation, general debility and heaviness, depression of spirits, loss of appetite, indigestion, faintness and sinking at the pit of the stomach, increased susceptibilities of the skin and the lungs to all atmospheric changes, feebleness of circulation, chilliness, headache, melancholy, hypochondria, hysterics, feebleness of circulation, feebleness of all the senses, impaired vision, loss of sight, weakness of the lungs, nervous cough, pulmonary consumption, disorders of the liver and kidneys, urinary difficulties, disorders of the genital organs, spinal diseases, weakness of the brain, loss of memory, epilepsy, insanity, apoplexy, abortions, premature births, extreme feebleness, morbid predispositions, and an early death of offspring.' If that wasn't enough, the author went on to warn his male readers that every ejaculation shortened their lives!

Gros Jos
When the time came to launch a leading brand of canned pork and beans in the Canadian market, the advertising company decided to continue the campaign that had worked successfully in other English-speaking areas, and retained the name Big John's. Canada is different, however. With a sizeable French-speaking population something was needed that would appeal to them as well, and the direct translation 'Grand Jean' seemed a bit tame. After some debate Gros Jos was settled on and the campaign team swung into action designing packaging, promotion and even a launch date. Only when a French-speaking

member of staff read the label did problems arise. She suggested that Gros Jos might be just a little too strong, even in French-speaking Canada, meaning as it does 'Big Tits'.

G-Strings

The highlight of a carnival held in the State of Virginia was a show modestly titled the *G-String Revue*. The four artistes that appeared in this not unnaturally attracted a large and appreciative audience, among them officers from the local police force who subsequently charged the four ladies with 'over exposure'. This was challenged by one of the defendants who maintained that she had never been on stage in a state of total nudity, as the police present maintained. She was adamant that she had been wearing her G-string at the time – round her ankle.

Frank Harris

The writer Frank Harris, best known for *My Life and Loves*, insured his card index of the 2,000 women he claimed to have seduced with Lloyd's. He was also the inventor of a pornographic card game he called 'Dirty Banshee' which included a pack of cards showing satyrs and goddesses enjoying a variety of sexual encounters.

Hays' Code

In 1930 the moral majority (not that it knew itself by that name in those days) hit back against what it saw as the growing licentiousness and depravity of the movie industry and introduced a production code that all film producers would be required to adhere to. Before filming started, all scripts had to be cleared by the office of the Motion Picture Producers and Distributors of America (MPPDA), headed by the conservative and all-powerful Will Hays. The Production Code Administration that was set under him to put the code into practice became one of the most influential bodies of the field of social mores, and the regulations themselves became dubbed the 'Hays' Code'.

Sex was the second principal category covered by the code — this is what it had to say on that subject as well as Vulgarity, Obscenity, Profanity, Costume and Dances:

The sanctity of the institution of marriage and the home shall be upheld. Pictures shall not infer that low forms of sex relationship are the accepted or common thing.

1 Adultery and illicit sex, sometimes necessary plot material, must not be explicitly treated or justified, or presented attractively.

2 Scenes of passion
   (a) These should not be introduced except where they are definitely essential to the plot.
   (b) Excessive and lustful kissing, lustful embraces, suggestive postures and gestures are not to be shown.
   (c) In general, passion should be treated in such manner as not to stimulate the lower and baser emotions.

3 Seduction or rape
   (a) These should never be more than suggested, and then only when essential for the plot. They must never be shown by explicit method.
   (b) They are never the proper subject for comedy.

4 Sex perversion or any inference to it is forbidden.

5 White slavery shall not be treated.

6 Miscegenation (sex relationship between white and black race) is forbidden.

7 Sex hygiene and venereal diseases are not proper subjects for theatrical motion pictures.

8 Scenes of actual childbirth, in fact or in silhouette, are never to be presented.

9 Children's sex organs are never to be exposed.

I. Vulgarity
The treatment of low, disgusting, unpleasant, though not

necessarily evil, subjects should be guided always by the dictates of good taste and proper regard for the sensibilities of the audience.

II. Obscenity
Obscenity in word, gesture, reference, song, joke or by suggestion (even when likely to be understood only by part of the audience) is forbidden.

III. Profanity
Pointed profanity and every other profane or vulgar expression, however used, is forbidden.

No approval by the production Code Administration shall be given to the use of words and phrases in motion pictures including, but not limited to, the following:
Alley cat (applied to a woman); bat (applied to a woman); broad (applied to a woman); bronx cheer (the sound); chip-pie; cocotte; God, Lord, Jesus, Christ (unless used reverently); cripes; fanny; fairy (in a vulgar sense); 'hold your hat'; louse; lousy; Mada (relating to prostitution); nance, nerts; nuts (except when meaning crazy); pansy; razzberry (the sound); slut (applied to a woman); S O B; son-of-a; tart; toilet gags; tom cat (applied to a man); travelling salesmen and farmer's daughter jokes; whore; damn; hell (excepting when the use of said last two words shall be essential and required for portrayal, in proper historical context, of any scene or dialogue based upon historical fact or folklore, or for the presentation in proper literary context of a Biblical, or other religious quotation, or a quotation from a literary work provided that no such use shall be permitted which is intrinsically objectionable or offends good taste).

In the administration of Section V of the Production Code, the Production Code Administration may take cognizance of the fact that the following words and phrases are obviously offensive to the patrons of motion pictures in the United States and more particularly to patrons of motion pictures in foreign countries:

Chink, Dago, Frog, Greaser, Hunkie, Kike, Nigger, Spic, Wop, Yid.

IV. Costume

1 Couple nudity is never permitted. This includes nudity in fact or in silhouette, or any licentious notice thereof by other characters in the pictures.
2 Undressing scenes should be avoided, and never used save where essential to the plot.
3 Indecent or undue exposure is forbidden.
4 Dancing costumes intended to permit undue exposure of indecent movements in the dance are forbidden.

V. Dances

1 Dances suggesting or representing sexual actions or indecent passion are forbidden.
2 Dances which emphasize indecent movements are to be regarded as obscene.

HEART BEATS

There's no doubt that sex gets your heart going. A number of surveys have shown pulse rates shooting up to rates between 142 and 150. In comparison the most vigorous athletic exercise seldom pushes the rate above 200, while the average at-rest pulse rate is between 60 and 70.

HELLO SAILOR

Sailors in the US Navy of the 1920s who returned from leave with more than they bargained for after dallying with the local ladies faced a set medical routine laid down in *The Medical Annual*:

In those who have been exposed to infection the entire penis is scrubbed with liquid soap and water for several minutes, and then washed with mercuric perchloride lotion 1:2000. Abrasions are sprayed with hydrogen peroxide. Two urethral injections of argyrol (10%) are then given and retained five minutes. The whole penis is then rubbed with 33% calomel ointment which is kept on for several hours.

ADOLF HITLER

When Soviet doctors carried out the autopsy on Hitler's partially burned body they could only find one testicle, lending credence to the popular wartime ditty that the German dictator was indeed deficient in this intimate area.

HOLDING BACK

Towards the end of the last century a Chicago physician, Dr Alice Stockham, advocated the practice of *coitus reservatus* in which a man inserts his erect penis into a partner's vagina but restrains from ejaculating. Dr Stockham was by no means the first to suggest this practice, but in spite of that her ideas met with bitter criticism from several fellow experts in the field. The advantages that she envisaged were: 'Manifestations of tenderness ... indulged in without physical or mental fatigue; the caresses lead up to connection (coupling) and the sexes unite quietly and closely. Once the necessary control has been acquired, the two beings are fused and reach sublime spiritual joy. The union can be slow controlled motions, so that voluptuous thrills do not overbalance the desire for soft sensations. If there is no wish to procreate, the violence of the orgasm will thus be avoided. If love is mutual, and if orgasm is sufficiently prolonged, it affords complete satisfaction without emission of orgasm. After an hour the bodies relax, spiritual delight is increased, and new horizons are revealed with the renewal of strength.'

HOLIDAY SNAPS
A chalet camp in East Anglia used to send out an application form for prospective visitors that requested, among other details, 'Number of children (by sex) ...'

One reply to this read, 'Three (and one by adoption)'.

HOLY FORESKINS
Not a turn of phrase that trips off the tongue of Batman's sidekick, Robin, but a reality, or seeming reality, in medieval Europe. The foreskin of Jesus Christ was once a leading religious relic in at least a dozen separate places in the Middle Ages. One such location was Abbey Church of Coulombs in the diocese of Chartres. The relic there was credited with making barren women pregnant and then relieving the pain of parturition. With modern medicines, not to mention the state of religion in contemporary France, time has moved on. The abbey lies in ruins today and its celebrated relic has disappeared without trace.

HOLY SEE
Today the Vatican rightly claims to be the country with the world's lowest birthrate; since most of its permanent residents are Roman Catholic clergy and nuns, the chances of a baby appearing in their midst are slim by anyone's reckoning. However, in the distant history of the Papacy this wasn't always the case.

Sergius III had an illegitimate son whom he arranged should succeed him as pope. In the middle of the tenth century John XII was accused of turning the church of St John Lateran into a brothel, though he was deposed following charges of incest and adultery. His successor, Leo VIII was little better; he died while committing adultery, the only pope known to have expired in this way.

Perhaps the most shameless of St Peter's successors was Roderigo Borgia, who styled himself Alexander VI. He had a string of mistresses and was an enthusiastic giver of wild parties. At one of these the Bishop of Ostia recalled the highlights of the evening when 'fifty reputable whores, not common but the kind called courtesans, supped ... and after supper they danced about with the servants and others in the place, first in their clothes and then nude ... chestnuts were strewn about and naked courtesans on hands and feet gathered them up, wriggling in and out among the candelabra ... Then all those present in the hall were carnally treated in public ...' To round off the evening the Pope awarded prizes to the men who had enjoyed the favours of the greatest number of dancers.

HONEY
No lesser authorities than Ovid, the Roman poet famed for his love poetry, and the Sheikh Nefzawi, the author of *The Perfumed Garden*, extolled honey for its aphrodisiac powers. As both a stimulus and ready source of energy, honey also has the distinction of being the only food made by insects that's eaten by man.

HOOVERS
Hoovers, vacuum cleaners, call them what you will, may be the answer to the houseworker's prayer but more unexpectedly they are also the source of unparalleled gratification for a surprising number of randy old men. Over a period of twenty years the *British Medical Journal* recorded several cases that required hospital treatment. There was a London man who was

apparently changing the plug on his Hoover (the 'Dustette' model) when the saucy little device inexplicably turned itself (and him) on and drew his most intimate parts into its innermost self. There was another elderly gent who was misguardedly hoovering a friend's stairs in nothing but a dressing gown when the attractions of the vacuum cleaner seduced him. Another victim of the household siren was a Colorado man who was ensnared while cleaning his car in his underpants. Apparently a build up of fluff (so to speak) clogged its workings and, as he sat to clean it on his lap, passion got the better of him.

HOUSEMAID
The *Press & Journal* carried an advertisement over half a century ago which read 'Wanted: Housemaid able to strip'.

HOWLERS
Ten classic schoolboy howlers that say more than they should:

1 'When a woman has many husbands, it is called Pollyana.'
2 'Abstinence makes the heart grow fonder.'
3 'In *Mrs Warren's Profession* her profession is the oldest profession, but she is not really a lost woman. She is just mislaid.'
4 'A virgin forest is where the hand of man has never set foot.'
5 'Cleopatra was famous for her beautiful open-toed scandals.'
6 'A polygon is another name for a Mormon.'
7 'When a man is married to one woman it is called monotony.'
8 'Oral contraception is when you talk your way out of it.'

9 'Cross-pollination is when the female flower is not in the mood.'

10 'The first commandment was when Eve told Adam to eat the apple.'

HUMAN PENIS: LARGEST

In the huge surveys carried out and documented in the Kinsey Report and substantiated by the results of a special *Forum* magazine survey into penis size, the largest recorded penises were ten inches and nine-and-a-half inches respectively.

HUMAN PENIS: SMALLEST

There are an awful lot of men who think that their penises droop some way short of the average size. To put things into perspective, the smallest penis encountered in the Kinsey survey was a mere one inch long. Medical literature quotes instances of penises that have barely reached half-an-inch when fully erect – organs that have been labelled with the somewhat insensitive but nevertheless appropriate term 'micro-penis'.

HUSBAND'S KNOT

Leaving aside questions of personal preference, physiologically no vagina can be too big for sex. The lining of the vaginal walls can be tightened by the use of astringents such as alum, and indeed in days gone by prostitutes used to use this to fake virginity for customers who were willing to pay an extra premium for the privilege of deflowering a virgin. Women who have had children will know that their vaginal muscles are slightly more relaxed after delivery, but they should remember that many men prefer space to move in and that sufferers of premature ejaculation will benefit from the more subtle stimulation of lax vaginal walls. Not so very long ago obstetricians used to perform a little tightening stitch called a 'husband's knot' which would narrow the vaginal opening and accelerate the return to vaginal taughtness. This has now been superceded by more postnatal exercises and physiotherapy.

HYPNOTISM

In 1864 the *Lancet* warned its medical readers about the dire sexual dangers that awaited women who allowed themselves to be hypnotized:

> The magnetizer [hypnotism was known as 'animal magnetism'] – independently of making the passes and of fixing his eye upon her – often takes her hands between his and then draws his fingers over various parts of her body, now over her face, and then over her body and legs, pressing, perhaps his knees against hers, and sometimes applying (we have seen this done) his lips to her stomach, and making insufflations upon it. Have we said enough to show that the use of animal magnetism is morally dangerous? We have heard it acknowledged by the most zealous practitioner of the art, that he has, more than once, witnessed all the excitement of action coition thus produced in a woman.

I LIBERTINE

I Libertine was one of those works of art that achieved a modest degree of popularity without ever existing. Ostensibly it was the life story of an eighteenth-century naval officer who'd whiled away his spare time documenting and researching contemporary erotica. In reality it was an idea put about by an American late-night disc jockey named Jean Shepard.

As the host of an all-night radio show, Shepard would commune with his insomniac listeners in a way that assured them that they, the 'night people', were the ones really in tune with life. To this end he suggested duping the dull 'day people' by creating a demand for a book that didn't exist – *I Libertine* was the outcome.

Word about it began to spread. A number of arts magazines ran articles on the author. *The New York Times* literary section listed *I Libertine* among forthcoming publications. One Columbia University student went as far as writing a paper on the novel and its author and was awarded a respectable grade.

By the time word got out that the whole thing had been a

spoof, there was a sizeable demand for the book and, rather than leave it at that, Jean Shepard was persuaded to write the book proper. When it appeared enthusiasm for the fantasy turned to indifference for the real thing.

IMAGINATION

Sexual fantasies have always been a powerful stimulus in the enjoyment of sex — even for professionals in the business. Mother Creswell, writing in *The Whore's Rhetorick*, had this advice for seventeenth-century aspirants:

> When you are detained in ugly, sordid, or ungrateful embraces, it would be difficult without the artificial aid of a picture to counterfeit those ecstasies which every comer may expect for his money. Therefore on these occasions you must frame in your mind the idea of some comely youth who pleases you best, whose shadow will create a greater lust than could be raised by a nauseous though real enjoyment. The picture of this charming boy may very fitly be placed near your bed, to imprint the fancy deeper in your imagination and enable you to fall into those sweet transports which do singularly gratify the enjoyer's heart.

IMPERIAL GREETING

When a former Chinese concubine succeeded to the throne of the Tang dynasty as the Empress Wu, she struck a note for feminism in more than political terms. Not only was she was the first woman ever to gain the imperial throne by her own machinations, she was also the first to institute the practice of official cunnilingus. Insisting that all her government officials and visiting dignitaries paid homage by 'licking of the lotus stamen', she would raise her gown whenever an official visitor appeared to permit him access to her imperial private parts.

IMPOTENCE

Sex researchers and therapists split impotence into three categories. There's incidental impotence which occurs from time to time when a man fails to get an erection after having had too much to drink, for example; or through tiredness, worry or anxiety.

More problematical is primary impotence which is the state attributed to men who have never had an erection substantial enough to permit vaginal entry. This is sometimes caused by physical conditions; serious diabetes can be a cause. If the condition has a psychological root, therapy is available with a very high success rate.

Between these two comes secondary impotence which occurs when men who once had satisfactory erections find that they no longer can. They too can be helped to return to their former prowess by following a step-by-step programme that takes the patient from one simple goal, like talking to a partner without progressing to necking, to the next (necking without petting), until he has the confidence and physical resources to achieve full and satisfactory penetration.

IMPROVING ON NATURE

Anthropologists in various parts of the world have found groups of men who have gone to remarkable lengths to modify and improve the sexual equipment with which nature endowed them. Men in Borneo were found to insert brass wire into the end of the penis as an added vaginal stimulus. Other materials like ivory and bamboo achieved the same ends. In nearby Sumatra, the Batak men went as far as deliberately slicing open their penises and inserting pieces of stone, which became firmly embedded as the wound closed over. These nobbly penises were also supposed to add excitement to love making – we can only hope that their ladies appreciated the gesture.

INDUSTRIAL ACTION
As part of a dirty jobs dispute staged by NUPE, six women staged a one-day token strike to register their protest by keeping their clothes on. The six normally spent their working week posing as nude models in the Manchester Regional College of Art.

INFIBULATION
As an operation, infibulation is just about as unpleasant in its consequences as it sounds. It first gained popularity in the ancient world where, in an effort to stop adolescent boys from masturbating, the foreskin was pulled over the end of the penis and held in place by a ring passed through a couple of specially pierced holes. It served the ancients well but as time went by infibulation dropped from regular practice and adolescents resumed theirs. Then a nineteenth-century professor of medicine in Germany hit on the idea as a way of stopping impoverished bachelors from fathering illegitimate children. Luckily for the bachelors his enthusiasm didn't catch on.

INNOCENTS ABROAD
As proof of the fact that filth is all in the mind, take the case of the American visitor who innocently falls prey to the vagaries of British vocabulary. Ordering 'two Bristols' when you want a couple of glasses of Harvey's Bristol Cream sherry can land a visitor in much the same embarrassment as assuming that 'cobblers' were the right people to mend shoes. How are Americans to know that to the vulgar British 'Bristols' are breasts (boobs/knockers/charlies/tits) and 'cobblers' are testicles (balls/bollocks/knackers/goolies)? Worse still is 'fanny' – a backside Stateside, but a female front-side in the British Isles.

English innocents are also inclined to refer to a rude sound of disapproval as a 'raspberry' and an idiot as a 'berk', without realizing that both these terms are based on Cockney rhyming slang, with 'raspberry' springing from 'raspberry tart' which rhymes with 'fart', and 'berk' coming from 'Berkley Hunt', which rhymes with 'cunt'.

You can try to restrict the use of written or spoken obscenities, but you cannot compel people to *think* clean. The corollary of not being able to force people to think clean is that you cannot force them to think dirty either. In 1959, fifty-one years after he intended it should be published, D. H. Lawrence's notorious novel *Lady Chatterley's Lover* made its unexpurgated appearance in the United States. The magazine *Field and Stream* published this delightfully tongue-in-cheek review which says all that needs to be said about innocence and incorruptibility:

> Although written many years ago, *Lady Chatterley's Lover* has just been reissued by the Grove Press, and this pictorial account of the day by day life of an English game-keeper is full of considerable interest to outdoor-minded readers as it contains many passages on pheasant raising, the apprehending of poachers, ways to control vermin and other chores and duties of the professional game-keeper.
>
> Unfortunately one is obliged to wade through many pages of extraneous material in order to discover and savour these sidelights on the management of a Midland shooting estate, and in this reviewer's opinion the book cannot take the place of J. Miller's *Practical Gamekeeping*.

INSECT REPELLENT

The Times of India reported the case of a striptease artiste in the coastal resort of Goa who had been sued by the management of the five-star Hotel Kalimpong, when she refused to undress during her performance at the hotel restaurant one evening. In her defence the artiste explained that this had only been caused by the persistent attention paid to her by mosquitoes that night.

INTERPRETING ART

When the bas-relief on a newly-opened post office was reviewed by *The Times*, the newspaper's art correspondent commented with some inspiration, 'The design consists of a male and female nude, recumbent, but with a suggestion that they are floating in water. Thus the main rhythms are not static, but suggest a movement of circulation appropriate to the transactions of the Post Office.'

IUD (INTRA-UTERINE DEVICE)

When an American woman was admitted to a hospital in France after being injured in a car crash, the doctors examining an X-ray of her abdomen noticed 'a cylindrical metal object ... bearing three linear appendages which ended in knobs'. Their immediate diagnosis was that the patient had swallowed her false teeth. However, the lady in question corrected this error, explaining that what they had seen on the X-ray was actually her 'pessaire anti-conceptionnel'. This baffled the doctors still further and they concluded that 'Social attitudes are decidedly curious on the other side of the Atlantic: prohibition is a state institution but people drink their fill behind closed shutters; everyone prides himself on his virtue but women wear pessaries against conception.'

INVASION THREAT

In 1798 the threat of military invasion from Napoleonic France had only just ebbed when the Bishop of Durham announced to a startled House of Lords that it had come to his attention that the only reason the enemy forces had backed away from military invasion was because they had hit on a more sinister method of bringing Britannia to heel. The plan, warned the Bishop, was to undermine the moral fabric of the nation by smuggling in hordes of ballet dancers.

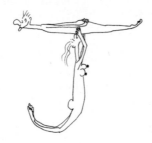

JOKING ASIDE
Five classic sexy stories:

1 Barely a fortnight away from their wedding a young couple offered to babysit the bride-to-be's younger brother while her parents spent the evening out having a well-earned break from the wedding preparations. Alone together they fell to tender embraces that rapidly shifted up a gear to heavy petting, and before long they had retired to the girl's bedroom for more adventurous fun and games. Only when they were both naked and in bed did the girl remember her mother's final request, to put on a load of washing. Worried that leaving it in the basket might suggest that she had been up to no good, the girl ran downstairs starkers with her boyfriend in hot pursuit, playfully offering to help. As they made their way through the dark a voice called out 'Surprise, surprise!' – and all the lights suddenly flashed on.

The girl's parents had arranged a surprise pre-wedding party for friends and relatives, with the vicar who was to marry them invited along as guest of honour.

(This story seems to have originated in North America half a century ago and it has been cropping up all over that continent ever since.)

2 A sixteen-year-old girl (they're always sixteen in this story) who had been having regular sex with her boyfriend, began worrying that he might lose interest in her if he had to keep wearing a condom. What she really wanted was to go on the pill, but as her doctor was a close family friend, she couldn't face asking him.

Then one day she found her mother's pills while tidying her bedroom and, not having a firm grasp of the principles of contraception, swapped these for aspirins.

The girl and her boyfriend were delighted by the new arrangement and they continued their happy sex life until a few months later when the *mother* announced that *she* was pregnant.

(This story has run and run in both North America and the UK, where is was printed as a true story in a national newspaper twenty-five years ago.)

3 A young man went downstairs early one morning wearing nothing but a short nightgown. As he was bending down to pick the post up off the mat he felt a cold hand on his exposed backside — little suspecting that it was the family dog giving him a friendly greeting. The shock was so great that the young man catapulted forward, straight through the glass panel in the front door and right into the street outside.

4 A jogger out for his early morning run passed a lone car parked by the side of the road, its windows all steamed up. Returning the same way half-an-hour later the car was still there and this time there were faint signs of life inside accompanied by pathetic cries for help. Peering inside he found a half-naked couple locked together in the backseat. The man, who was on

top, told him that his back had gone and he couldn't move. The jogger ran off to call the police. The police arrived, took one look and called the fire brigade. A fire crew arrived, took one look and summoned an ambulance. A quick consultation between these two agencies resulted in the top being cut off the car so that the injured man could be lifted free.

'I'm sorry about this, lady,' said the senior fireman as the lady's lover was driven away to the casualty department, 'but at least he hasn't come to any more harm this way.'

'To hell with him,' she replied, 'How am I supposed to explain to my husband what's happened to his car?'

(This tale has a special popularity in the UK, where the vehicle in question is always a Mini, though versions have cropped up in Australia and the USA.)

5 A boss who was expecting a quiet birthday with his family at home was taken completely by surprise when his highly desirable secretary invited him back to her home for a drink after work. Hoping against hope that she was giving him the come-on at last, he readily accepted. Back at her place she offered him a large whisky and then said that she just had to slip into the bedroom to see to a few things. Well, how much more of an invitation does a man need than that? In an uncharacteristic burst of impetuosity, the boss tore off his clothes and was standing in his socks when the bedroom door opened and his wife, children, colleagues and several friends rushed into the room with a big birthday cake, all singing 'Happy Birthday to you ...'

JOYOUS LIFE-AFFIRMING STATEMENTS
This was how a Florida man described the graffiti with which he defaced a couple of hundred public library books over a three year period between 1977 and 1980.

Among his contributions the self-styled 'sex enthusiast' numbered:

The word for the day is legs – spread the word!

Be nice to boobs; they outnumber people two to one.

Librarians make novel lovers.

The second greatest sin in the world is to turn away from your lover when you know they want sex. The greatest sin in the world is to have sex when you don't want it.

The most beautiful girl in the world has got spots on her ass.

If you're feeling horny, smile at the librarian.

All lollipops don't have the same flavour.

Fuck Jane Austen.

After commenting that not all the defendant's statements appeared to be of a similar literary merit, the judge fined him $2,000.

JUDICIAL RULINGS

A senior judge, hearing a plea for damages made on behalf of a twenty-five-year-old man who claimed that his sex life had been seriously affected by an accident with a bulldozer, asked whether the plaintive was married. He replied that he wasn't. In that case, argued the judge, how could the accident possibly affect him?

JUST DESERTS

The marked difference between the public and private lives of medieval priests was highlighted by the case of a Spanish cleric who was found guilty of rape, consorting with prostitutes, extorting sexual favours in exchange for absolution — not to mention committing blasphemy. As punishment he received thirty days house arrest and a two-ducat fine!

JUST FILMZ

Jason Irwin of Chicago was a man with entrepreneurial flair. Realizing the kicks that many men get out of listening to women mouthing obscenities, he set up a unique telephone service to cater for the need and gave it the name Just Filmz Inc. Fifteen dollars bought callers twenty minutes of non-stop filth from a talking hostess of the caller's choice. For an additional five bucks she did the talking topless. Finding hostesses posed no problems by all accounts. Former telephone operators fitted the bill perfectly — 'They're naturals' claimed Mr Irwin.

JUSTINE

According to the Marquis de Sade (and he should have known), Justine was a lady who more than merited her name. She it was who entertained the Marquis and three of his friends simultaneously. While de Sade busied himself with Justine's backside, Antonin 'made an offering to the contrary God'. Meanwhile, Jerome was pleasuring her mouth, while Clement set to work between her hands.

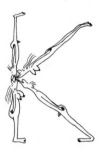

Karezza

Karezza was the technique described in Sanskrit and Hindi sexual treatises whereby men remained with erect penises inside their partners for hours on end, without reaching a climax themselves. This is not a technique restricted to India. There are accounts in Chinese literature and official records of busy mandarins attending to more than one job at once, so to speak. While happily pleasuring concubines for several hours, they were apparently able to sign documents brought to them and even discuss urgent matters with visitors, with only the occasional movements from down below to make sure that they remained erect in connection with the other matter to hand.

Karnak

There is an ancient monument at Karnak in Egypt which carries the most detailed and probably most extensive example of the 'unkindest cut of all', when King Menephta took awful revenge on a Libyan army he defeated around 1300 BC. As the record states, he brought home an impressive collection of penises, cut from his foes:

Phalluses of Libyan generals	6
Phalluses cut off Libyans	6,359
Sirculians killed, phalluses cut off	222
Etruscans killed, phalluses cut off	542
Greeks killed, phalluses presented to the king	6,111

KEEPING IT UP

The duration of erections varies with age, as the following table shows:

AGE	DURATION
16–20	43 minutes
21–25	54 minutes
26–30	53 minutes
31–35	47 minutes
36–40	41 minutes
41–45	31 minutes
46–50	29 minutes
51–55	22 minutes
56–60	27 minutes
61–65	19 minutes
66–70	7 minutes

KERB CRAWLING

An ordinance passed in the city of Abilene, Texas decreed:

It shall be unlawful for any person to idle or loiter on any street or thoroughfare, sidewalk, or alley, or in any store, theater, motor car, motion picture show, business house, or in the entrance or doorway of any place within the corporate limits of the city of Abilene for the purpose of plying the avocation of flirt or masher.

It shall further be unlawful for any man to stare at or make googoo eyes at, or in any other manner look at or make remarks to or concerning, or cough or whistle at, or do any other act to attract the attention of any woman upon or travelling along any of the sidewalks, streets, public ways of the city of Abilene with an intent or in a manner calculated to annoy such women.

ALY KHAN

Aly Khan, son of the late Aga Khan is famed as one of the greatest lovers this century. Accounts of his sexual prowess have been dismissed by sceptics, but those who knew him better maintain that he was able to exercise extraordinary self-control when making love, so that sex several times a day with different women was perfectly feasible. The suggestion was that as a youth Aly had been sent to learn the oriental technique of *imsak* with the result, according to a close friend, that 'No matter how many women Aly went with, he seldom reached climax himself. He could make love by the hour, but he went the whole way himself not more often than twice a week ... Otherwise his life would not have been possible, because he only thought of that every night, and every day too.'

Apparently his chauffeur used to have instructions to drive very slowly through Hyde Park when his employer had a lady companion in the back of his Rolls-Royce. This ensured there was time to make to love to her, an activity that would frequently fill the time as he moved from one lady's home to another's.

The Kinsey Report

The publication of Alfred Kinsey's report on the sexual practices of the human male in 1948 attracted its fair share of opprobrium. One complainant wrote to say that this milestone in the study of human sexuality was nothing more than a complete waste of time and simply confirmed the writer's conviction that 'the male population is a herd of prancing, leering goats'.

The Kiss

As one of Rodin's most celebrated works, The Kiss did not find favour with public opinion in the USA in the 1880s, which decided that the nude marble sculpture was far too hot for public viewing and had it confined to a special room.

LADIES ONLY

Against the backcloth of conventional Victorian prudery, the writer and publisher Mary Wilson stood as a champion for women's sexual liberation. Theresa Berkley (she of the brothel famous for the variety of its flagellation equipment) called her 'The reviver of erotic literature in the present century'. In addition, Mary Wilson was also a keen campaigner for women's brothels and contributed an essay to *The Voluptarian Cabinet* on this subject under the title *Adultery on the Part of Married Women, and Fornication on the Part of Old maids and Widows defended by Mary Wilson, Spinster, with Plans for Promoting the same, Addressed to the Ladies of the Metropolis and its Environs.* Her scheme envisaged a palatial brothel for women only – a sanctuary 'to which any lady of rank and fortune may subscribe, and to which she may repair incog; the married to commit what the world calls adultery, and the single to commit what at the tabernacle is called fornication, or in a gentler phrase, to obey the dictates of all-powerful Nature, by offering up a cheerful sacrifice to the

God Priapus, the most ancient of deities.' Sad to say, her plans never progressed beyond this draft stage.

LARD
One of the more unexpected erotic ointments can apparently be made from mixing lard with crushed and strained garlic.

LAST WILL AND TESTAMENT
William Shakespeare left his wife his 'second best bed', and an industrialist from Philadelphia who died in 1947 included among his bequests, 'to my wife I leave her lover, and the knowledge that I wasn't the fool she thought I was'.

From more recent times comes the will left by a Yorkshire vicar who viewed his daughter's adherence to contemporary fashion with mounting horror. All the same he left her the majority of his considerable fortune when he died – but with one stipulation:

> Seeing that my daughter Anna has not availed herself of my advice touching the objectionable practice of going about with her arms bare to the elbows, my will is that, should she continue after my death this violation of the modesty of her sex, all goods, chattels, moneys, land, and other that I have devised to her for the maintenance of her future life shall pass to the oldest of the sons of my sister Caroline.
>
> Should anyone take exception to this my wish as being too severe, I answer that licence in dress in a woman is a mark of a depraved mind.

D H Lawrence

In 1930 the great liberating novelist of human passions wrote in *Pornography and Obscenity*, 'Masturbation is certainly the most dangerous sexual vice that a society can be afflicted with in the long run.'

Legion of Decency

In the October of 1934 the Catholic Charities Convention held a meeting in New York City at which one of the speakers was Monsignor Amleto Giovanni Cicognani. 'What a massacre of innocence of youth is taking place hour by hour!' he harangued his audience. 'How shall the crimes that have their direct source in the immoral motion pictures be measured?' he asked, before declaring, 'Catholics are called by God, the Pope, the Bishops and the priests to a united and vigorous campaign for the purification of the cinema, which has become a deadly menace to morals.'

With that speech, he laid the foundation for the Legion of Decency which came into being a year later with the main function of rating films according to moral classifications.

Anyone wishing to join the League in 1934 took this pledge (later to be revised in 1965):

> I wish to join the Legion of Decency, which condemns vile and unwholesome moving pictures. I unite with all who protest against them as a grave menace to youth, to home life, to country and to religion.
>
> I condemn absolutely those salacious motion pictures, which, with other degrading agencies, are corrupting public morals and promoting sex mania in our land.
>
> I shall do all that I can to arouse public opinion against the portrayal of vice as a normal condition of affairs, and against depicting criminals of any class as heroes and

heroines, presenting their filthy philosophy of life as something acceptable to decent men and women.

I unite with all who condemn the display of suggestive advertisements on billboards, at theatre entrances, and the favorable notices given to immoral motion pictures.

Considering these evils, I hereby promise to remain away from all motion pictures except those which do not offend decency and Christian morality. I promise further to secure as many members as possible for the League of Decency.

I make this protest in a spirit of self-respect and with the conviction that the American public does not demand filthy pictures, but clean entertainment and educational features.

Let Justice Be Done

The old divorce laws which once sat on the statute books were viewed with contempt even by many of those who made their living from them. Mr Justice Maule pointed out the absurdity of them when he came to his summing-up at the end of a trial for bigamy:

Clerk of Assize: 'What have you to say that judgement should not be passed upon you according to the law?'

Prisoner: 'Well, my Lord, my wife took up with a hawker and ran away five years ago: and I have never seen her since, so I married this other woman last winter.'

Mr Justice Maule: 'Prisoner at the Bar, I will tell you what you ought to have done, and if you say you did not know, I will tell you that the Law conclusively presumes that you did. You ought to have instructed your attorney to bring an action against the hawker for criminal conversation with your wife. That would have cost you £100. When you had recovered substantial damages against the hawker, you would have instructed your attorney to sue in the ecclesiastical courts for a divorce *a mensa et toro*. That would have cost you £200 or £300 more. When you had obtained a divorce *a mensa et toro*, you would have had to appear by counsel before the House of Lords for a divorce *a vinculo matrimonii*. The Bill might have been opposed in all its stages in both Houses of Parliament, and altogether you would have had to spend about £1,000 or £1,200. You will probably tell me that you never had 1,000 farthings of your own in the world, but, prisoner, that makes no difference. Sitting here as a British judge it is my duty to tell you that this is not a country in which there is one law for the rich and another for the poor.

LETTUCE
According to Andrew Boorde, the author of the first English book of domestic medicine (his *Dyetary*) lettuce was to be avoided at all costs by anyone who valued his or her sex life. As the good doctor wrote, 'Lettyse doth extynct veneryous actes'. Figs, on the other hand, could be guaranteed to 'stere a man to veneryous actes, for they doth urge and increase the sede of generacyon'.

LIP SMACKING
The appearance and size of the inner and outer lips of the vagina will vary greatly from one woman to another. They may be openly on display, or totally hidden by pubic hair. Both sets of lips may increase in size considerably during sexual arousal.

Among certain groups living in southern Africa the labia can be as long as seven inches and the owners of such equipment have to push the lips back into the vaginal opening in order to get on with their daily tasks.

LITERARY BROTHEL
When the Reading Room opened its doors for the first time in the city of St Louis, Missouri, it became the world's first literary brothel. In return for the salon's fee, clients discovered that they could be entertained by nude hostesses whose sole task was to read them pornographic or erotic literature.

LONELY HEARTS
The first woman to place a lonely-hearts advertisement in a British newspaper was Helen Morrison, a spinster of Manchester. Her plea for companionship appeared in the *Manchester Weekly Journal* in 1727. She got an answer soon enough – the city's mayor confined her to a lunatic asylum.

LORD CHAMBERLAIN'S OFFICE
Until its demise 1968 the Lord Chamberlain's Office carried out some remarkable acts of censorship on the British stage. Among those to cause greatest amusement were:

There must be no scratching of private parts. (*Meals on Wheels*, by Charles Wood)

The Doctor's trousers must *not* be hauled down. (*The Happy Haven*, by John Arden)

The statue of President Johnson must not be naked. (*Mrs Wilson's Diary*, by Richard Ingrams and John Wells)

LOST AND FOUND
The medical profession have long since ceased to be shocked or surprised at the wide variety of objects which continue to be extracted from the vagina. Various 'lost' but still vibrating dildos have been retrieved, as have whole unpeeled oranges. On one

occasion a broken length of broom handle found its way up through a perfectly innocent household accident and remained undetected until the housemaid in question went to her doctor with curious vaginal discharge. A GP in the south of England also reported treating a patient complaining of a more sinister vaginal discharge, black in colour. A quick examination put her at ease but may have done little for her embarrassment; the culprit was a misplaced liquorice all-sort.

Others make a positive virtue of extending the range of vaginal activities beyond the most sought after. Not long ago a performer in Paris won some notoriety for employing her vagina to swallow, and then powerfully eject, table tennis balls and the history of the seamier side of nightlife around the world is littered with accounts of vaginas that have played harmonicas or smoked cigarettes.

LOST BALL

Several years ago the *Daily Mail* considered the best way of dealing with a flasher on a golf course and received in reply a letter which ran:

I read with interest of the lady golfer who, when confronted by a naked man wearing only a bowler hat, asked him whether he was a member, and then hit him with a Number 8 iron.

Purists will long dispute whether it was obviously a mashie-shot, or whether the niblick should have been used. I hold no strong views myself, but I do wonder what the lady would have done had the man produced from his bowler hat a valid membership card.

Love Dish

The American sexologist, Professor J L McCary, devised a pudding which seemed to have all the best attributes of an effective aphrodisiac. This consisted of sliced pears and strawberries soaked in Cointreau and covered with a sauce of beaten egg yolks, confectioner's sugar, cloves and cinnamon.

As the professor commented, 'The dessert is smooth, rich and creamy in texture – qualities we subconsciously equate with sexuality. In addition, its redolence (cloves, cinnamon, liqueur) is "exotic", another word we tend, however vicariously, to identify with sexual concepts.'

Love: life and death

A court in Cleveland, Ohio was told of the extraordinary inventiveness, not to mention athleticism, that coloured the sex life of Dr David Love and his wife Virginia who, on at least three occasions, made love hanging from a window of their fourth floor apartment. Tragically the rope tied around Mrs Love's ankle slipped from her husband's grasp and she fell to her death. He was subsequently charged with involuntary manslaughter, although his lawyer was quick to point out that 'Whatever happened certainly doesn't indicate that Dr Love is guilty of anything.'

Love Locked Out

In the fifteenth century, a chastity belt that really worked appeared on the European market. This was the brainchild of Francesco de Carerra, a senior legislator in Padua, and it amounted to a padlock that closed the vaginal labia tight by the simple expedient of passing right through them – or as it was more decorously phrased at the time 'locked up the seat of voluptuousness'. The device remained popular for a century after its invention, finding particular favour in France, where, according to one account, it sold so quickly at a fair in Paris that the stallholder was hustled out of town by the young men of the city who saw their favourite quarry rapidly being locked away.

LOVER'S LEAP

When Vera Czermak found that her husband had been unfaithful, her first thought was to throw herself out of the window of their third-floor flat in Prague and put an end to her misery. With a tragic irony she very nearly succeeded. Leaping from the window sill she fell directly on top of a passer-by walking along the pavement below. Mrs Czermak received only a few cuts and bruises but her victim was killed instantly. To her amazement (and do doubt his) he turned out to be her miscreant husband.

LSD

Timothy Leary, high priest of the drug culture, was once interviewed in *Playboy*. When the conversation turned to sex the interviewer asked, 'We've heard that some women who ordinarily have difficulty achieving orgasm find themselves capable of multiple orgasms under LSD. Is that true?'

'In a carefully prepared, loving LSD session,' answered Leary, 'a woman can have several hundred orgasms.'

'Several hundred?!'

'Yes. Several hundred.'

Magnetic Powers

Anyone in late eighteenth-century London who was anxious to 'insure the removal of barrenness' or 'improve, exalt, and invigorate the body and through them the mental faculties of the human species', need not have looked further than the Temple of Health where Dr James Graham had constructed what he modestly termed his 'medico-magnetico-musico-electrical bed'. This offered its occupants seventy-two square feet of invigorating repose on a mattress stuffed with the tail hair of leading stallions. Surmounted by a mirrored dome, Dr Graham's invention was supported by twenty-eight glass pillars and was encircled by 1,500 pounds of lodestones 'so as to be continually pouring forth in ever-flowing circles inconceivable and irresistibly powerful tides of the magnetic effluxion, which is well-known to have a very strong affinity with the electric fire.'

The result of all this, according to the good doctor, were, 'strong, beautiful, brilliant, nay, double-distilled children.'

But just in case the bed failed to live up to his claims, Dr Graham wisely installed a more familiar sexual stimulus in the form of Emily Lyon, who took the form of Hygeia and danced naked for the clientele. She later became better known as Lord Nelson's mistress, Lady Hamilton.

MALE ORDER
A bomb disposal squad was called to the main postal sorting office in the French port of Le Havre after one of the postmen on duty detected a sinister ticking inside a parcel he was handling. The young lady to whom it was addressed was asked if she could account for it and, covered with confusion, gave her explanation and sent the bomb men on their way. Inside the parcel was a battery-operated vibrator that had somehow become switched on during transit.

MALE ORGASMS
It may come as a shock to most men, but pre-adolescent boys are more likely to have a higher orgasm rate than the mature members of their sex. From his observation of 182 pre-adolescent boys Alfred Kinsey noted the following results:

Rate of Successive Orgasms	Number of Boys
Once	81 out of 182 (44.5%)
Twice	17 out of 182 (9.3%)
Three, four or five times	42 out of 182 (23.07%)
Six to ten times	30 out of 182 (16.48%)

Topping the list was an outstanding twenty-one orgasms in a row.

The only compensation for the adult male is that these feats are generally lost when the orgasm is accompanied with ejaculation of semen.

MANDRAKE

Mandrake is one of the oldest aphrodisiacs still in use. It is mentioned in the Old Testament and Pliny likened its appearance to human genitals, which can only have helped its amatory cause. Mandrake comes from the same family as the potato (once thought to be endowed with aphrodisiac powers itself). It has small red fruit and large, dark brown leaves.

MARITAL SEX

In general terms younger married couples have sex more often than older couples – as might be expected. Figures compiled over a number of years revealed frequency rates of:

Couples ages 18 to 24	twelve times a month.
Couples ages 25 to 34	eight to eleven times a month.
Couples aged 35 and older.	eight times a month or less.
Couples aged 45 and older.	about four times a month.

Among couples of all ages, the frequency of intercourse looked like:

Never	2%
Less than once a month	8%
Two to four times a month	47%
Two to three times a week	31%
Four or five times a week	12%

Massage Parlours
Back in 1973 the Turin vice squad had a tip-off that all was not as it should be in one of the city's massage parlours which offered a variety of therapeutic services, among them 'Overall body massage with opportunities for meditation'. By means of the passwords 'Peace and goodwill' the squad broke in and caught a considerable number of clients red-handed, red-faced and red in several other places as well. Among the frolicking number was a Catholic priest discovered stark naked and coupled in 'deep meditation' with a nubile masseuse – all in the line of duty, or so he made out, 'I needed this experience to understand the problems of my parishioners.'

Mice
According to one obscure belief in ancient Rome, smearing mouse excrement over someone made them impotent.

Mixed Bathing
Sixty years ago mixed bathing was only allowed in the Council swimming baths at Bradford-on-Avon if the bathers were related.

Marilyn Monroe
Marilyn Monroe was born Norma Jean Mortenson and spent a deprived childhood during the Depression in a home, deserted by her father shortly before she was born. Deprived of a stable relationship with either parent, she lived in a fantasy world with dreams of financial and social success. She stood on the threshold of that world when war broke out and she went to work in a factory; it began to open up for her when a photographer first spotted her and the camera became her true love. Ambitious to make it to the top, she divorced her first husband, became one

of the country's leading models and in 1946 had her first screen test with Twentieth Century-Fox. Voluptuous yet vulnerable, she was put through the studio's star-grooming routine from which she emerged as the screen phenomenon known to the world as Marilyn Monroe.

Sex played an important part in her public and private life. She described the Hollywood of the late 1940s as 'an overcrowded brothel' but was no stranger to the casting couch herself. In spite of her enormous popularity and the huge attraction she held for men throughout her life she remained incredibly insecure. She apparently told her sometime lover, Marlon Brando, 'I don't know if I do it right' and Norman Mailer, another to enjoy her favours, was quoted as saying that the screen goddess was 'pleasant in bed, but receptive rather than innovative'.

When she signed her first big contract, Marilyn reputedly said, 'That's the last cock I'll have to suck', though at the same time she seemed to be looking around for greater conquests.

By most people's standards Marilyn Monroe was fairly uninhibited; bathing infrequently, and belching and farting with carefree abandon. She did, however, bleach her pubic hair and delighted in wearing no underwear.

Frank Sinatra (another of her liaisons) introduced her to the Kennedys, and the prospect of working her way into the uppermost levels of American political life appealed to her enormously. 'Can you imagine me as the First Lady?' she asked a friend in 1962. Secret rendezvous with the President were not long in following in locations that ranged from Beverly Hills, his brother-in-law's beach house and the presidential jet. Her persistent phone calls and the risk of public disclosure unsettled Jack Kennedy and he was happy to pass Marilyn over to brother Bobby, who apparently consummated their relationship parked in a car outside the same brother-in-law's beach house in Santa Monica.

Towards the end of her life Marilyn Monroe was becoming

increasingly unstable emotionally, consuming a growing quantity of medicaments and attending frequent psychiatric counselling sessions. Death from a drug overdose was the conclusion reached after she committed suicide, though speculation existed that she might have been murdered.

Following her death her second husband, the baseball player Joe DiMaggio, arranged for fresh roses to be delivered to her grave three times a week.

MORAL POLLUTION
In 1975 the Festival of Light announced plans for creating a hostel in London to treat 'victims of moral pollution'. It was planned that pornography addicts, sexual deviants and 'others involved in erotica' would pursue compulsory spiritual activities and take courses in handicrafts. The estimated cost was in the region of £3,000 per inmate, though the residents would be expected to make contributions towards the overheads through sick benefit or social security payments.

MULTIPLE BIRTHS
There is a plaque on the wall of an abbey near the Hague which records a strange event that took place in the thirteenth century:

Margaret, daughter of the illustrious Lord Florent Count of Holland and Mathilde, daughter of Henri Duke of Brabant, Sister of William, King of Germany, being forty-two years of age, was delivered on the Friday before Easter, at nine o'clock in the morning, in the year 1276, of 365 babies male and female which (in the presence of several great lords and gentlemen) were arranged in front of the font and were all baptized by a bishop, the males being christened the same name, namely Jean, and the females Elizabeth. All died soon after, as did the mother, and all were buried in the same sepulchre.

Modern medical thinking suggests this might have been due to what is commonly known as a 'bunch of grapes pregnancy'.

MUSIC TO MAKE LOVE TO
A dozen sexy song titles to take you all the way:
  1 I Want to Hold Your Hand — Beatles
  2 Kiss Me Honey Kiss Me — Shirley Bassey
  3 Hanky Panky — Madonna
  4 Let's Get Physical — Olivia Newton-John
  5 Let's Spend The Night Together — Rolling Stones
  6 Je T'aime (Moi Non Plus) — Jane Birkin and Serge Gainsbourg
  7 Be Stiff — Devo
  8 Anyway You Want It — Dave Clark Five
  9 Give It To Me Now — Kenny
  10 Give Me An Inch — Hazel O'Connor
  11 Bring It On Bring It On — James Brown
  12 Ain't No Stopping Now — McFadden Whitehead

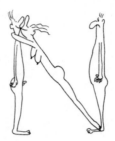

Naked Animals

One morning in 1959 viewers to the American television show *Today* were introduced to a man with a remarkable mission. His name was G Clifford Trout Jnr and his self-appointed task took the form of a crusade for animal and human welfare, by imposing morally acceptable standards for the nation's livestock. 'Don't let your moral standards go lower and lower due to naked animals', he told the interviewer. 'It's a shocking situation, and I am spending every single minute of every single day and every last dollar of my father's money to correct this evil.'

To this noble end Mr Trout had founded the Society for Indecency to Naked Animals. Visitors to its New York head-quarters were confronted with pictures of both domestic animals and livestock all discreetly shielding their private parts with a variety of strange garments. *Life* magazine featured the society in an article that also showed a number of household pets similarly garbed.

Public opinion was pretty evenly divided. Half the population thought Dr Trout was yet another crank, confirming that the nation was steadily slipping towards mass lunacy. While the other half supported the society's worthy aims; one wealthy admirer even offered a donation of $400,000, which had to be declined as outside donations were apparently prohibited according to the terms under which SINA had been established.

Like many earnest campaigns, the society raised moral indignation over a period of three years when a 'naked' papier mâché horse was put on display in a Manhattan airline office; the horse was quickly removed and an apology was sent as speedily. Mr Trout was active on a personal level and was pictured in the *San Francisco Chronicle* trying to dress animals in the city zoo.

Only when Mr Trout and his associate, Mr Alan Abel received the accolade of an interview with America's top television journalist, Walter Cronkite, did SINA disappear from the limelight. Mr Cronkite's associates in the network saw what others had failed to notice – Mr Trout was actually an unemployed actor and former colleague named Buck Henry. SINA had been an inspired hoax dreamt up by the imaginative Mr Abel (of whom more presently).

NAKED TRUTH
One Saturday night in the summer of 1966 police in Brooklyn apprehended sixteen teenagers of both sexes aged between sixteen and nineteen who were dancing naked in the street. When they appeared in the dock they constituted the largest number of people ever to appear stark naked in a court room. After hearing that they had been attending a high school graduation party, they were released by the judge on the condition that they were each driven to their parents' home exactly as they appeared in court – with only a blanket for cover.

NAME CHANGES

Name changing is a regular feature in the entertainment business – sometimes for obvious reasons. Marti Caine was once Lynda Crapper; Jane Wyman was Sarah Jane Faulks and Diana Dors was Diana Fluck.

According to showbiz folklore the latter caused serious problems for a vicar in her home town who was delighted when the rapidly rising starlet agreed to return to open his church fête. Miss Fluck had not long changed her name to Miss Dors, and anxious to make her feel at home, the vicar decided to call her by her old name – though he was scrupulous in remembering to include the all-important L. 'Ladies and gentlemen,' he began when the great moment arrived, 'I am going to ask you to welcome a very special person here this afternoon. She is known to the world as Diana Dors. She is better known to us of course as Diana Clunt.'

NATIONAL CHARACTERISTICS

The result of one limited survey of penis lengths carried out by Dr Robert Chartum showed that of the five European groups measured the longest in each group (as classified) was:

Group	Penis Length
1 English	$10\frac{1}{2}$ inches
2 West German	$8\frac{1}{2}$ inches
3 Danish	8 inches
4 Swedish	$7\frac{3}{4}$ inches
5 French	$7\frac{3}{4}$ inches

While the smallest penises in each of the national groups were:

1 Danish	5 inches
2 Swedish	5 inches
3 French	$3\frac{1}{2}$ inches

| 4 West German | $3\frac{1}{2}$ inches |
| 5 English | $2\frac{3}{4}$ inches |

NATURISM

During the Second World War a nudist village for evacuee naturists was set up twenty miles outside London. Accommodating mainly mothers and children, the village had a warden and first-aid post and included tuition in basic skills like cooking (with special emphasis on careful use of the frying pan) 'in the altogether'. The residents were confident that wartime experience would convert many more of their clothed countrymen to shed their garments too — presumably for no other reason than that it eased the problems caused by clothes rationing.

NEVER ON A MONDAY

According to one survey conducted in France, only one per cent of Frenchmen have enough energy left after the weekend to have sexual intercourse on Monday nights.

NOCTURNAL SEX

The human preference for sex after dark seems at odds with nature. In much of the animal world night is the time set aside for sleep — pure and simple. Sex takes its place in the daytime routine along with hunting, eating and grooming. Similarly testosterone, the sex hormone secreted by the testes, is produced in its greatest quantities during the morning; it tails off markedly come nightfall.

Not Tonight

Even in an age of permissiveness not every boy–girl encounter ends up between the sheets. A survey conducted among college students gave these reasons – first for men not going to bed with their companions:

1	Fear of pregnancy	22%
2	Unable to talk girl into it	21%
3	Not their decision	14.5%
4	Didn't love the girl	14%
5	Worried about worsening relationship	11%

... then for women not going to bed with their boyfriends:

1	Didn't love him	37%
2	Thought it was morally wrong	16%
3	Fear of pregnancy	16%
4	Fear of feeling ashamed afterwards	15%
5	Worried about worsening relationship	11%

Novels

O S Fowler, author of *Sexual Science* (1875), offered this warning against the sexually dangerous practice of reading novels:

> Novel reading redoubles this nervous drain begun by excessive study. What is or can be as superlatively silly or ruinous to the nerves as that silly girl, snivelling and laughing by turns over a 'love story'? Of course it awakens in her Amativeness. In this consists its chief charm. Was there ever a novel without its hero? It would be *Hamlet* played without Hamlet. Yet how could depicting a beau so heroic, lovable and dead in love, fail to awaken this tender passion in enchanted readers? To *titillate Amativeness*, mainly, are novels written and read. For this they

become 'vade mecums', and are carried to table, ride, picnic, walk, everywhere. It is doubtful whether fiction writers are public benefactors, or their publishers philanthropists. The amount of nervous excitement, and consequent prostration, exhaustion, and disorder they cause is fearful. Girls already have ten times too much excitability for their strength. Yet every page of every novel redoubles both their nervousness and weakness. Only Amazons could endure it. Mark this reason. Amativeness, that is, love, and the nervous system, are in the most perfect mutual sympathy. Love-stories, therefore, in common with all other forms of amatory excitement, thrill. In this consists their chief fascination. Yet all amatory action with one's self induces sexual ailments. It should always be with the *opposite* sex only; yet novel reading girls exhaust their female magnetism without obtaining any compensating male magnetism, which of necessity deranges their entire sexual system. The whole world is challenged to invalidate either this premise or inference. Self-abuse is worse, because more animal; but those who really must have amatory excitement will find it 'better to marry' and expend on real lovers those sexual feelings now worse than wasted on this its 'solitary form'. Those perfectly happy in their affections never read novels, because *real* love is so much more fascinating than that described.

Nude Calendar

The world's first nude calendar appeared in 1913 and very demure it was too. The subject was a prize-winning painting by the French artist Paul Chabas, entitled *September Morn*, which showed a winsome maiden standing naked, but modestly so, by the sea in the morning mist. However, the president of the Anti-Vice League in the USA, the notorious Anthony Comstock, did not approve, complaining, 'There's too little morn and too much maid'.

Nude Conjuring

The idea may defy the commonly accepted principles of the art of conjuring but fifty years age there was a small and enthusiastic group of nude conjurors. *London Life*, covering a party held by the National Sun and Air Association, went into some detail in describing the magician Mr Tony Alexander, who, despite his absence of clothing, managed to produce cards and handkerchiefs from thin air and won himself a round of applause – and a five pound bet into the bargain.

Nude Statue

The first nude statue to be unveiled in London was the work of Sir Richard Westmacott and showed the Greek warrior Achilles in all his manliness; a subject that had been chosen to represent the all-conquering powers of the Duke of Wellington, who seven years earlier had trounced the French at Waterloo. Great as his victory had been, London was not quite ready for a twenty-foot high anatomically accurate Achilles, especially as the statue had been commissioned and paid for by the grateful women of England. Within a few days of its unveiling Achilles was modestly kitted out with a fig leaf.

OBSCENE GESTURES

Flying in his hang-glider one sunny day a South African by the name of James Barthes, spotted a young woman sunbathing in the nude on her rooftop and made an obscene gesture at her as he glided overhead. Unfortunately for him, the lady's husband had also spotted his illicit signalling from the bedroom and grabbing his machine-gun he went to the window and shot the hang-glider pilot and all out of the sky in a hail of bullets.

OBSCENE PUBLICATION

In 1708 the first trial prompted by the publication of allegedly obscene material came before a British court. The offending title was *Fifteen Plagues of a Maiden-Head* which the court found obscene but not punishably so. A short time later it had a change of heart, however, and indicted the publisher-cum-bookseller Edmund Curll for selling *Venus in the Cloister, or the Nun in her Smock* which was a spicy tale of lesbian nuns, first published in France in 1682.

OBSCENITY COMMITTEES

In accordance with a Supreme Court ruling that returned powers of censoring pornographic films to local communities, the town of Clarkstown, New York, established a nine-member 'obscenity committee' under the chairmanship of Harry Snyder. While bringing many qualities to his new post, Mr Snyder could not be said to possess great insight into the subject — in fact he didn't possess any sight at all; the new chairman was registered as blind.

Local reporters were keen to know how he managed to carry out his civic duties, to which Mr Snyder replied blithely that fellow committee members sat beside him during screenings and gave a running commentary 'to fill me in when the screen goes silent'.

OH CALCUTTA!

When *Oh Calcutta!* opened in Stockholm there was more of a stir caused outside the theatre on the first night than on the stage, when six members of the audience turned up stark naked to take their seats. Feeling more put out than embarrassed when the theatre management turned them away, the six complained that they had understood that 'you had to be in the nude in order to get in'.

OLYMPIC GAMES

The *News of the World* called it 'The most shocking sporting event ever to be screened' and newsmen from around the world hurried to interview the organizers of the Sex Olympics when it was announced that these very contemporary games were due to be staged in 1971.

The spokesman for the organizing committee was one Dr Harrison Rogers, who explained that like the more orthodox Olympic movement, the new games were to be truly international in flavour. Adjudication would be undertaken by a panel of distinguished doctors and psychiatrists and, to the delight of the press, he went on to say that the finals would be screened worldwide.

Beside Dr Rogers at the press conference was an attractive blonde woman, who was introduced as one of the competitors. In the best traditions of international competition she emphasized the importance of playing the game for its own sake.

In reply to one question, 'In track it's the legs that go first, would you say ...', she interrupted with a modest, 'I don't know. I haven't been competing that long.'

The press conference ended – well, almost ended – with the screening of some of the 'heats'. After these, Dr Rogers took the assembled company completely by surprise by peeling off his false beard and revealing himself as Alan Abel, hoaxer extraordinary.

What they'd just seen was an excerpt from his full-length film *Is There Sex After Death?*, a blue movie parody that he'd made on a very tight budget – so tight in fact that the only way he could think of promoting it was to call a press conference – of a sort!

ON HEAT

Memphis, Tennessee must have been a lively place for the city's policemen in the early 1970s. By her own admission in front of a grand jury, Charlotte Tyler, a nineteen-year-old housewife admitted to having slept with around 5,000 officers of the force! Not through choice, she insisted, and this was the nub of her case, but because of an unfortunate accident. 'I am bringing an action for $1,000,000 against a health spa,' she told the court. 'There, trapped for ninety minutes in the sauna, I changed from a devout Catholic housewife into a raving nymphomaniac.'

She explained her appetite for policemen as 'something to do with my belief in law and order' and rested her hopes in an attorney who specialized in 'shock-induced behaviour switch'; he had recently won damages of $300,000 for a client left similarly afflicted after a cable car crash.

ORAL SEX

Twenty years is a long time in the development of sexual experience. Back in the 1950s when Alfred Kinsey carried out his pioneering work very few married couples (in America at any rate) practised oral sex of any sort. Two decades later, the situation in the permissive 1970s had changed drastically:

1 Marriages in which oral sex was practised   60%
2 Married couples aged under 35 who practised oral sex   80%
3 Married people aged under 25 who had experienced oral sex   90%
4 Men who performed cunnilingus   75%
5 Married women who performed fellatio on their husbands   43%

ORGASM: CAUSES OF FIRST EXPERIENCE FOR WOMEN

1 Masturbation   40%
2 Intercourse   27%
3 Petting   24%
4 Dreaming   5%
5 Homosexual encounters   3%
6 Psycho-sexual stimuli   1%

ORIENTAL SCRUPLES

In 1926 China became the first country in the Far East to permit kissing to be shown on its cinema screens. Across the sea in Japan things were viewed differently. There kissing was deemed by some in positions of authority to be 'unclean, immodest, indecorous, ungraceful and likely to spread disease'. As a result, while Chinese audiences were relishing every passionate embrace in 1926, Japanese censors that year systematically snipped 800,000 feet out of imported foreign films.

DUKE OF ORLEANS
Philippe, Duke of Orleans, brother to the future Louis XIV was raised as a girl to ensure that he wouldn't pose a threat to his elder sibling's claim to the throne of France. The somewhat drastic treatment worked. Philippe never lost his childhood orientation and was known to lead his troops into battle in high heels and wearing a perfumed wig. According to his wife 'he was more afraid of the sun, or the black smoke of gunpowder, than he was of musket balls'.

OVERHEATING
When the hot tub craze swept through California in the late 1970s middle-aged Wesley Laroya and his wife Helen were quick to get in on the action. With the tub installed in their Simi Valley home the happy couple indulged in regular fun and games in it, with never a thought for their high blood pressure. One evening in May 1979 they eagerly clambered in after warming up with several glasses of favourite tipple, turned the thermostat up high and set to. The next morning their bodies were found in the tub where they had fallen asleep.

OYSTERS
Most shellfish and a good many sea fish besides are reckoned to possess impressive aphrodisiac qualities but none more so than the oyster. Rich in phosphorus, it is easy to digest and acclaimed by lovers of great experience, like Casanova who

regularly breakfasted on a couple of dozen and extolled them as 'a spur to the spirit and to love'.

PENIS: ARTIFICIAL

In 1977 a female student at the University of Missouri became the first patient to be turned from a woman to a man by means of surgery. As evidence of his/her new status, the patient was fitted with an artificial penis capable of having an erection. As *The New York Times* informed its readers, 'The doctors said the penis contained a tiny hydraulic system that permitted a fluid to be pumped from a reservoir in the abdomen into the penis to cause erection.'

PENIS CAPTIVUS

One of the more distressing consequences of sex without serenity is a rare, but no less alarming condition that prevents withdrawal when all is done and spent. This seems to be caused by a powerful muscular spasm in the vagina that locks the erect penis fast and bonds the amorous couple like Siamese twins. In such a state understandable anxiety sets in and the situation deteriorates. From the early years of this century comes an account of one such episode that occurred in the docks of Bremen. 'A great crowd assembled,' runs the report in *The Sexual*

Life of Our Time, 'from the midst of which the unfortunate couple were removed in a closed carriage, and taken to the hospital, and not until chloroform had been administered to the girl did the spasm pass off and free the man.'

PENIS ENVY

As far as most women are concerned the only enviable thing about a penis is the ability it confers on the owner to pee out of a coach window as it powers along a motorway when the bladder feels like bursting and the driver refuses to stop. On the other hand (or should it be 'in the other hand'?) men believe that the penis is in some way a magical and versatile instrument that all men are proud to possess and all women should be desperate to acquire. The truth, not surprisingly, is very different. Women soon learn that with their anatomy and a modicum of allure they can have as many penises as they want.

Whether you have a penis of your own, or are just sharing one, the story of Eleanor Wainwright is sobering. When she complained to a doctor that it was down below freezing she could not have been nearer the mark.

Against all medical advice a large and well-known British oil company had decided to break through time-honoured barriers of sex discrimination and employ this spunky lass, a liberated young lady and somewhat vociferous champion of equal rights for women, as their first ever female labourer. There was nothing wrong in that, except that Eleanor had little idea about the conditions awaiting her on the construction site in Alaska. There the company had undertaken to lay some thousands of miles of pipe line across the permafrost, spreading before it specially constructed polystyrene boards to guard against the disastrous consequences of direct contact with the ice. So it was that Ms Wainwright found herself manhandling (if that's the word) the seven-by-four polystyrene boards across the frozen Alaskan wastes, often in the teeth of gale force winds and in temperatures down to -40°C.

For the first couple of days this was stirring stuff – until practical difficulties began to take their toll. When God in his wisdom chose not to bless women with the same convenient appendage through which men pass water, he left them with little choice but to strip off and squat. Anticipating this difficulty for their new employee, the oil company installed an incinerator loo which, at the press of a button, was triggered into fiery life as six flame-throwing nozzles squirting blazing diesel in all directions enveloping and consuming all that lay in its path. Efficient as it undoubtedly was, the incinerator loo wasn't for the workforce who feared the menace it posed to their privates.

Poor Eleanor was no exception. But unlike her workmates her privates were threatened in other quarters. Despite soldiering on for three days she finally admitted defeat when frostbite of the labia majora forced her to abandon the job.

She won her subsequent litigation but as far as penis envy goes, it was a bitter experience.

PHYSICAL DECLINE

There is an element of truth in the belief that too much sex can curve your spine and rot your bones. One complication of non-specific urethritis leads to ankylosing spondylitis, a disorder whereby the vertebrae of the spine become fused in a fixed, rigid bamboo-like structure. Sufferers become bent and stooped and are subject to respiratory difficulties as their chests are compressed by the curvature. Furthermore, long-standing un-treated gonorrhoea and syphilis cause joint swelling and inflamm-ation with the gradual erosion of complete joints in severe cases.

Edith Piaf

Edith Piaf was born to destitute parents in one of the seediest districts of Paris. They soon deserted her and the little girl was left to be raised in the house of ill repute run by her grandmother. Fired by an intensely feminine and creative energy, she was spotted as a teenager by her first impresario, who snapped her up off the streets where she had been making her living and introduced her to the torrid cabaret life of the French capital.

Because she looked like a sparrow, for which the French slang is 'piaf', she soon adopted the name and from then on was known by nothing else. She was four foot ten and described herself as having sagging breasts and a low-slung bottom. She had no illusions about her physical attractions; what drew men to her was the power of her personality.

Her background made her an early starter in the love stakes. She was interested in men from every walk of life and divided her lovers into those from the streets, sailors, pimps, flings, professors and factory workers. Her sheer emotional and physical energy nevertheless took its physical toll, and at various times in her life she abused alcohol and drugs as well as notching up a significant number of car accidents of varying degrees of seriousness.

'You never know a guy until you have tried him in bed. You know more about a guy in one night in bed than you do in months of conversation,' she once said. There was, however, one man she regarded perhaps more highly than any other, and that was the retiring, talented and very muscular boxer Marcel Cerdan, who unfortunately already had a wife and three sons. Her love for him was intense and her sense of loss was as great when he was tragically killed in a crash on the way to visit her in New York a matter of months after winning the world middle-weight title; Piaf had persuaded him to make the trip.

Although it took her months to get over Cerdan's death, Edith Piaf's desire for other men finally conquered her grief and according to her sister, Momone, 'she went wild, she ate her heart out, she was jealous and possessive ... she howled and she locked guys up'. For her part Piaf once told her sister, 'You can't have a house without a man, Momone, it is worse than a day without sunshine.'

Piss
'Piss' is one of several four-letter words less acceptable today than it has been in the past. A hundred years ago a 'piss-maker' was a great drinker; to 'piss one's tallow' meant to sweat; a 'vinegar-pisser' was a miser; to 'piss out of a dozen holes' was to have syphilis; and to 'piss when one can't whistle' was to be hanged. Even today, lukewarm wine of an inferior quality drunk by an alcoholic actor could be colloquially described as 'a piss-artist's piss-warm gnat's piss'.

Pizzle
In days gone by flogging was not simply a matter of being whipped or beaten with a variety of canes — the pizzle was also available as an instrument of punishment. A quick investigation in a dictionary reveals that this curious sounding device started life as a bull's penis. Due to its generous proportions it was put to use on malefactors after its original owner had no further use for it.

Pornography
The word 'pornography' comes from the Greek meaning 'the writing of prostitutes'.

POTATOES
When the potato was first introduced into the British diet it was regarded as being an aphrodisiac.

PROSTITUTION
There is no evidence that prostitution existed as a sole source of income for its practitioners in the earliest forms of human society, among the so-called hunter-gatherers. The 'oldest profession' probably didn't come into being until man had started settling into agricultural communities around 15,000 BC. And it wouldn't have been until the development of the first cities that streetwalkers really started to come into their own 11,000–12,000 years later.

PROVOKING THE DESIRE
Ten tipples to temptation:

1 Between the Sheets
   $\frac{1}{3}$ brandy
   $\frac{1}{3}$ white rum
   Shake
   $\frac{1}{3}$ cointreau
   1 dash of lemon juice

2 Bosom Caresser
   $\frac{2}{3}$ brandy
   $\frac{1}{3}$ orange curaçao

   Shake
   1 yolk of egg
   1 teaspoon of sugar syrup

3 Cupid's Bow
   $\frac{1}{4}$ gin
   $\frac{1}{4}$ Forbidden Fruit liqueur
   Shake
   $\frac{1}{4}$ aurum (or curaçao)
   $\frac{1}{4}$ passion fruit juice

4 Fallen Angel
   $\frac{3}{4}$ gin
   2 dashes crème de menthe

$\frac{1}{4}$ fresh lemon or lime
juice
Shake

1 dash of angostura
bitters

5 First Night
$\frac{1}{2}$ brandy
$\frac{1}{4}$ Van der Hum
Shake

$\frac{1}{4}$ Tia Maria
1 teaspoon of cream

6 Honeymoon
$\frac{1}{3}$ Benedictine
$\frac{1}{3}$ calvados

Shake

$\frac{1}{3}$ lemon juice
3 dashes of orange
curaçao

7 Maiden's Prayer
$\frac{3}{8}$ gin
$\frac{3}{8}$ cointreau
Shake

$\frac{1}{8}$ orange juice
$\frac{1}{8}$ lemon juice

8 Playmate
$\frac{1}{4}$ brandy
$\frac{1}{4}$ apricot brandy
$\frac{1}{4}$ Grand Marnier
$\frac{1}{4}$ orange squash
Shake

white of egg
dash of angostura
twist of orange peel

9 Roberta May
$\frac{1}{3}$ vodka
$\frac{1}{3}$ aurum
Shake

$\frac{1}{3}$ orange juice
$\frac{1}{2}$ teaspoon of egg white

10 Temptation
$\frac{7}{10}$ rye whisky
$\frac{1}{10}$ orange curaçao
$\frac{1}{10}$ Pernod
Shake

$\frac{1}{10}$ Dubonnet
twist of orange peel
twist of lemon peel

Psycho-kinetics

Uri Geller caused a sensation with his strange, unexplained powers to bend metal. However, it was not only household cutlery that fell under his all-powerful, all-twisting spell. Miss Sigrid Hemse, spinster of Gotland, Sweden fell foul of Mr Geller in a most unexpected way when she discovered that she was pregnant. Uri had no personal knowledge of the event. He had been appearing on television at the time. But Miss Hemse maintained that his psycho-kinetic powers had bent her contraceptive device while she and her fiancé were making love as they watched him on television.

Pubic Hair

For most people their 'short and curlies' remain that way. However, sexual history records remarkable cases of feminine pubic hair that has grown to be longer than the hair on the owners' heads. In one case it stretched to below a woman's knees and in another the pubic hair was gathered into a tasteful plait that reached behind her back.

Pubic Haircuts

Twenty years ago trend-setting Mary Quant hit on pubic hair as the fashion motif for a new age and had her own trimmed into a tasteful heart shape. 'We shall move towards exposure,' she duly prophesied, 'and body cosmetics and certainly pubic hair will become the fashion emphasis, if not necessarily blatant.'

Pussies Galore

Twenty names for female genitalia:

Pussy	Cockpit
Crumpet	Quim
Cunt	Growler

Fanny

Snatch

Where the Monkey Sleeps

Love Tube

YMCA

Twat

Gash

Muff

Snatch

Bearded Clam

Moonlit Mile

Hole

Bush

Twitcher

Vagina

QUARTERBACK LIBIDO

This has nothing directly to do with the overt sex drives of American footballers, or the claim of the early Hollywood starlet Clara Bow that she once 'entertained' the whole of the University of Southern California football team in rapid succession.

No – this springs from deeper, some might say primeval roots. In fact the first person to say it was anthropologist Thomas Hornsby Ferril, who wrote an article in the Rocky Mountain *Herald* in December 1955 that put forward the idea that American football is actually a:

> ... syndrome of religious rites symbolizing the struggle to preserve the egg of life through the rigours of impending winter. The rites begin at the equinox and culminate on the first day of the New Year with festivals identified with bowls of plenty; the festivals are associated with flowers such as roses, fruits such as oranges, farm crops such as cotton, and even sun-worship and appeasement of great reptiles such as alligators.

Warming to this theme, Ferril suggests that the 'egg of life' is symbolized by the oval inflated bladder of pigskin and by the oval-shaped outdoor arenas to which worshippers flock in their thousands in search of 'an outlet from sexual frustration' which they hope to find in the 'masochism and sadism' displayed before them by a highly-schooled 'priesthood of young men'.

Examining the field of play, Ferril sees the green of the grass as a symbol of summer, overlaid by white stripes representing the snows of winter. Then there are the 'semi-nude virgins' who move in carefully choreographed, ritualized patterns on the fringes of the field and the frenzied chanting of the worshipping onlookers, all of which is overlaid with the 'Oedipus theme of willingness to die for love of Mother', or Alma Mater, to give the deity its more familiar institutional name.

Although, as Ferril readily admits, many of the rites performed by the 'twenty-two young priests of perfect physique, might appear to the uninitiated as a chaotic conflict concerned only with hurting the oval by kicking it', the pattern of worship is highly stylized. Looking at the formation into which the priests with the egg go, he focuses on the central priest — the quarterback:

> Actually ... the 'quarterback' symbolizes the libido, combining two instincts namely (a) Eros, which strives for even closer union and (b) the instinct for destruction of anything which lies in the path of Eros. Moreover, the 'pleasure-pain' excitement of hysterical worshippers focuses entirely on the actions of the libido-quarterback. Behind him are three priests representing the male triad.
>
> At a given signal the egg is passed by sleight-of-hand to one of the members of the triad, who endeavours to move it by bodily force across the white lines of winter ... At the end of the second quarter, implying the summer solstice, the processions of musicians and semi-nude virgins are resumed ... The virgins perform the most curious rites

requiring far more dexterity than the earlier phallic May-pole rituals from which it seems to be derived. Each carries a wand of shining metal which she spins on her fingertips, tosses playfully into the air, and with which she inter-weaves her body in most intricate gyrations ...

Like so many folk customs, the reality of what is seen on the superficial level is obviously a little different. As Dussie Nell Davis, a US majorette coach, commented almost twenty years ago, 'Sex is a word I have never used with my girls and I never will. Sure, I tell them that when they're out on the field I want them to forget that they're Momma's little girls and *project*! After the game, they're Momma's little girls again.'

QUESTIONS OF CONTRACEPTION
The popularity of different contraceptive methods varies from country to country. Estimates based on data collated from UK sources suggests that British lovers find these the most popular methods:

Contraceptive	Users
1 Condom	39%
2 Oral contraceptive	27%
3 Withdrawal	25%

On the other hand there seem to be few who favour:

Contraceptive	Users
1 Rhythm method	6%
2 Cap	6%
3 Spermicides	5%
4 Coil	5%

QUICKTIME

Most men take less than six minutes from the time of entry to the time they ejaculate. Certain techniques perfected and mainly practised in the Orient enable some men to hold out almost indefinitely, but most Western men seem unable to break beyond the six-minute barrier. About one in four reckon they're good for ten minutes, though just under one in five admit to ejaculating in less than two minutes.

Statistics like these do not compare well with the animal world where the male rattlesnake apparently lasts twenty-four hours before letting himself go. No wonder Eve was seduced by one of his predecessors.

QUININE

Quinine, taken in the evening, is reckoned in Iran to be a useful aphrodisiac.

RABBITS

A British delegate to a teachers' convention on sex education held in the United States, posed the question, 'Why have sex education in our schools? I was brought up before the era of sex education and I managed to get by. Don't forget, there is not a rabbit warren in the land where they show sex education films and yet this has never been a problem for the rabbits of the world. Indeed, those of you who are of a literary bent will recall that Peter Rabbit was not an only child. There was Flopsy and Mopsy and Cottontail as well as Peter. And doubtless there would have been many more had it not been for that unfortunate accident which befell Mr Rabbit in Mr MacGregor's garden whereby he ended up in one of Mrs MacGregor's rabbit pies. Doubtless Beatrix Potter felt it was a neater finish to the story than a vasectomy.'

RAINDANCING

Faced with a national drought that was playing havoc with his own garden and those of his village neighbours, one Richard Bullock took matters into his own hands and ended up in the dock for his pains. 'I was brought up in Nigeria,' he explained to the court, 'and when the consequences of the drought became obvious I decided to put the national interest first and perform the *n'dula*, a naked rain dance, on the village green. That night the rain began and continued for twenty-four hours. I estimate that up to £500,000 worth of crops were saved.'

Taking a less sanguine view, the court fined him ten pounds.

RASPUTIN

The son of a Siberian farmer, Rasputin soon adopted the motto 'work hard and play hard', especially when it came to drink and women. It was said that nature had endowed him with a penis some thirteen inches long and an insatiable sexual appetite – so much so that even in his teens his physical attributes were the delight of many local girls. At sixteen he was seduced by the beautiful wife of a Russian general and then by her six handmaids one after the other. From then on there was no looking back. By the time he was twenty Rasputin had married a local girl and before long had sired four children.

At the beginning of this century he joined the rather weird religious sect known as the Khlist, which cleaved to the belief that in order to receive absolution it was necessary to sin first. Flagellation and other exotic practices formed part of its creed and Rasputin entered into the spirit of these with enthusiasm. By 1905 he had moved to St Petersburg where his growing reputation as a miraculous healer brought him to the attention of the Czar and Czarina. At court, Rasputin's influence grew after his beneficial intervention in the treatment of their hae-mophiliac son. The Khlist was the perfect vehicle with which to secure the acceptable seduction of vulnerable women, and the message he propounded of redemption through sexual release resulted in hundreds of guilt-ridden and frustrated women falling prey to his advances; his bedroom soon became known as 'the Holy of Holies'.

By 1916 Rasputin's influence at court had become intolerable for the old guard Russian aristocracy. A group of vengeful noblemen invited him to dine with them one evening, served him poisoned food and wine and then set about murdering him – a process that was anything but straightforward. As he slipped into unconsciousness, Rasputin was apparently sexually assaulted by one homosexual murderer, who then spitefully shot him four times. As he lay dying, he was castrated by another who threw his severed penis across the room where it was snapped up by a servant and hidden. Passed to a maid, the penis remained in her custody for over half a century, lovingly preserved in a polished wooden box. In 1968 the lady was traced to her home in Paris where Rasputin's splendid organ was still intact and resembling a well-ripened banana about a foot in length.

READING THE FACE

Two thousand years ago a sex manual written in China laid down a few guidelines for gauging a woman's sexual characteristics from a careful study of her face. It had some interesting things to say:

> A woman with a small mouth and short fingers has a shallow *porte feminine* and she is easy to please. You can be sure that a woman must have big and thick labia if she has a big mouth and thick lips. If she has deep-set eyes her *porte feminine* is bound to be deep too ... if a woman has a pair of big, sparkling eyes, her *porte feminine* is narrow at its entrance, and yet roomy in the inner part ... A woman with two dimples is tight and narrow down below ...'

RELAXED PENIS

How big is the average relaxed penis? Four inches long and four inches around – take a tape measure and check for yourself. In actual fact 90 per cent of penises range from three to five inches in length, but dimensions change with prevailing conditions. Jump into a cold swimming-pool, for example, and who can blame your frozen phallus from shrinking away to a delightfully compact inch or so.

In the same way it knows enough to tuck itself well out of harm's way in the face of physical threat, so becoming a much smaller target for an irate wife with a meat cleaver who suspects it of getting exercise elsewhere.

Conversely, warm weather, convivial surroundings and sexual activity a short time before measurement will all temporarily increase the resting size of the organ.

REVENGER'S TRAGEDY

When Anna May Reese took a new lover her estranged husband was seized with murderous jealousy. Knowing that she was used to entertaining the new man in her life in her bedroom, her former bedmate slipped into the house while she was away and hid a stick of dynamite between the mattress and the bed springs. From this he ran a fuse through the floor and out of an air vent into the garden outside. After seeing the lovers return to the house, he listened with an ear to the wall until he heard them getting down to bedtime matters and then, in the words of firework manufacturers, lit the blue touch paper and retired. Meanwhile the couple in bed were so engrossed in each other that neither of them heard the fuse as it spluttered towards them. Anna May was under her boyfriend when the fuse reached the explosive and was blown into the next world. He escaped with a couple of burned hands.

RIVETER'S OVARIES

During the summer of 1943 when wartime industrial production in the USA was nearing its peak, a wave of absenteeism swept through women working in key areas of the US war effort to the extent that the FBI were called in to investigate whether some elaborate form of Axis sabotage was afoot. They confirmed, and other investigators corroborated it, that workers were being driven from their lathes and benches by wholly fictitious sexual fears. Some worried that they were gradually being made sterile by welding equipment or the ultra-violet and infra-red rays to which they were exposed. Others worried that riveting led to cancer of the breast. The same occupation also gave rise to the popularly termed 'riveter's ovaries' — another mysterious condition with no founding in medical science. There was fear of pregnancy as well, especially among women who filled aircraft fire-extinguishers. A rumour ran through their number that the carbon tetrachloride with which they worked would have the same effect as too intimate a connection with the servicemen on whose behalf they were working to supply the equipment.

ROAD SAFETY

In an attempt to curb speeding motorists on a stretch of highway in Pennsylvania, the local police erected a sign that read 'Caution — Nudists Crossing'.

ROUGH MUSIC

Many folk songs are packed with euphemisms of sexual encounters some of which are scarcely disguised, as in the American 'shanty', 'While Strolling Through Norfolk':

> While strolling through Norfolk one day on a spree,
> I sighted a packet, her sails flowing free.

She was broad in the counter and bluff in the bow;
She flew the tricolour; her gaskets hung low.

Chorus
Singing, faldi I aldi I, singing faldi I aldi I, faldi I aldi I faldi
I ay.

I ran up a signal, a signal she knew.
She backed her main topsail and for me hove to.
I hailed her in English, she answered, 'I ay'.
She was from The Blue Anchor, bound for Tigers Bay.

I broke out my bow chaser and for her I bore,
And yardarm to yardarm, along we just tore.
We sailed along fleetly, both meekly and sweet,
And when we dropped anchor, 'twas on Avon Street.

Behind a breakwater, from storms well insured,
In a snug little harbour, she soon had me moored.
She furled up my mains'l, my tops'ls and royals,
Put her lily white hand on my boom tackle falls.

I inspected her locker, found plenty of room,
And down in her oarlock I stowed my job boom.
She yawed with her sternsheets, both ample and wide,
And at me let fly with a ringing broadside.

Well, I fought with the Russians, the Prussians also,
And I've fought with the Limeys and Johnny Crapaud,
But of all the damn fighters I ever did see,
She reminded me most of that stinkpot Chinee.

JOHN RUSKIN
For all his appreciation of art in its many forms, John Ruskin
was a complete wreck when it came to his sex life. On his
wedding night the sight of his wife's pubic hair so appalled him
that he was shocked into sexual abstinence for the rest of his

life — not that he lost the urge. In place of orthodox intercourse he became an addicted masturbator indulging in 'a suicide committed daily'. He kept a diary of his sex dreams but died a virgin.

RUTTING

In his study of a herd of red deer F F Darling noted that during the autumn rutting season stags used their antlers to masturbate. This, he observed, 'is accomplished by lowering the head and gently drawing the tips of the antlers to and fro through the herbage. Erection and extrusion of the penis from the sheath follow in five or six seconds ... Ejaculation follows about five seconds after the penis is erected ...'. He goes on to remark that a few minutes later the same antlers could be in use with the animals full weight behind them as they slash and batter those of an opposing stag.

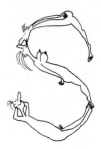

The Marquis de Sade

The notorious Marquis de Sade got his kicks from inflicting pain — on others as well as on himself (sado-masochism). He was imprisoned by royal decree for staging orgies at which he whipped and sodomized women. He despised homosexuals, and although there were plenty of other sexually depraved aristocrats around at the time, he was unfortunate enough to have married into a family (the Montreuils) who had strong court connections, and it was they who made sure that he was jailed, partly to get him off their backs (so to speak) and partly as an example to others.

When he was imprisoned in 1768 for sexual sadism he managed to secure an early release by the devious means of getting his wife pregnant while she visited him in jail. Having secured his freedom, his sexual appetite continued unabated and he threw himself into an even more vigorous life of carnal debauchery. On one occasion he sent his faithful valet, La Tour, to procure four waterfront prostitutes. Once inside the Château de la Coste they were subjected to a complex orgiastic ritual involving beatings and floggings interspersed with an endless variety of anal and vaginal intercourse. The prostitutes, all aged between eighteen and twenty-three, apparently became La Tour's perks and he was generally expected to join in the fun as well. Unfortunately at least a couple of the girls overdosed on Spanish Fly, a powerful aphrodisiac which caused violent and uncontrolled vomiting in addition to its furiously libidinous effect. This brought a swift end to the Marquis's exploits and he and La Tour had to go into hiding for the next few years.

As generally happens, his mother-in-law finally caught up with him and, having obtained a special licence from the Court, arranged for him to be imprisoned for twelve years. Here he discovered his most enduring sources of sexual pleasure — pornography and masturbation.

SEWING MACHINES
An article published in the USA in 1867 under the title *The Influence of Sewing Machines on Female Health* warned against the inherent dangers of seamstresses becoming sexually aroused by the constant motion of the foot treadle, and advised the use of bromide to counteract any improper stimulation.

SEX — TWENTY-FOUR 'SEX-' WORDS TO BE IDENTIFIED
The three letters S-E-X don't always mean what immediately springs to mind, as the following show when you try to match the words with their definitions — answers on page 178.

The Words	Definitions
Sextuple	Occurring every six years
Sexavalent	Relating to sixteen.
Sexfid	A stanza of six lines.
Sextoncy	A period of six years.
Sexennium	A bronze coin of the Roman Republic.
Sexennarian	A long fishing boat propelled by six oars.

Sextans	To multiply by six.
Sexen	Having six fingers.
Sexvirate	Measured by sixty degrees.
Sexfoil	Having a chemical valency of six.
Sexagene	Of six thousand years.
Sexto	The office of a sexton.
Sexdigital	Sectarian.
Sextipartition	Piece of paper cut six to a sheet.
Sexagenary	A six-year-old child.
Sexagecuple	Having six leaves.
Sexious	Divisions into sixths.
Sexcuple	Proceeding by sixties.
Sexadecimal	Six-fold.
Sexennial	Multiplied by sixty or a power of sixty.
Sexdigit	A body of six colleagues.
Sexmillenary	Divided into six segments.
Sextain	Based on the number sixty.
Sextile	A person with six fingers.

SEX AND DRUGS

Staff at the medical centre at Heathrow airport once called in the Customs and Excise after discovering that two men admitted in a critical condition had brought it upon themselves after swallowing a total of forty-eight condoms filled with liquid cannabis.

SEX EDUCATION IN SCHOOLS

The first English school in which sex education was formally given was Abbotsholme School whose first headmaster, Cecil Reddie, introduced the idea in the autumn term of 1889. His aims were 'to prevent mental illusions due to false ideas from within and to prevent false teaching from other fellows'.

Reddie divided his pupils into three broad bands for the purposes of instruction in this innovative subject. Youngest of the three were the 'Pre-Puberty' boys aged ten to thirteen; they were to be taught 'the true facts of their origin, of their life development, and of the dangers that surround them ...'. Above them were the 'During-Puberty' pupils aged thirteen to sixteen whose curriculum was to include 'the laws of the feelings they now experience ... it is best at this period that they should think as little as possible about these matters'. Finally Reddie addressed himself to the 'After-Puberty' group for sixteen- to twenty-year-olds. They were to be instructed in 'the laws of later life, so that they will enter the world equipped on this point'.

Few educators outside the school showed any enthusiasm for adopting Reddie's pioneering ideas. However, they also escaped the severe censure that might have been expected from the high-minded moralists who strutted busily through the Victorian England of his day.

SEXERCISE

Making love burns up more calories than playing golf and not that many fewer than throwing a frisbee. This is how it shaped in a list of ten activities:

Activity	Calories burned up
1 Gym workout	200–820 per hour
2 Cycling	200–600 per hour
3 Roller-skating	200–500 per hour
4 Dancing	300 per hour
5 Throwing a frisbee	200 per hour
6 Making love	150 per hour
7 Playing golf	133 per hour
8 Walking (slowly)	115 per hour
9 Playing cards	100 per hour
10 Flying a kite	30 per hour

Sex Offenders

There is an assumption that sex offenders have abnormally large penises. Like a lot of popular assumptions on the subject, this is wrong. The Kinsey researchers compiled data on sex offenders and found that the estimated penis length of exhibitionists was not unusual. In fact the penis of a sex-murderer, Dewitt Clinto Cook was 'so tiny that he and his wife were forced to satisfy one another orally'.

Sexual Symbols

A list of regularly-occurring dream objects that are accepted by psychoanalysts as sexual symbols produced 102 symbols for a penis and just over half that number for sexual intercourse itself.

The Sheik

Rudolph Valentino's celebrated performance in the 1921 film *The Sheik* was epoch-making both for his career and for the depiction of love scenes on the silver screen. When the olive-skinned Valentino was seen kidnapping a white girl and taking her to his tent where he seduced her, cinema audiences were treated to a franker exposé of naked lust on the screen than they had ever seen before. As the script for the seduction scene ran, 'She withered in his arms as he crushed her to him in a sudden excess of passion. His head bent slowly down to her, his eyes burned deeper and, held immovable, she endured the first kiss she had ever received. And the touch of his scorching lips, the clasp of his arms, the close union with his warm, strong body robbed her of all strength and of all power of resistance.'

SISTINE CHAPEL

Recent restoration of the ceiling of the Sistine Chapel has revealed once more Michelangelo's awe-inspiring masterpiece. Sadly not every one of St Peter's successors has been as appreciative of his work as they might have been. Pope Paul IV, for instance, was so shocked by what he saw that he ordered the work to be obliterated in 1555 on the grounds of obscenity. This blanket condemnation brought an outcry of popular protest and a compromise was reached whereby all the naked figures in *The Last Judgement* were to have clothes painted on them. Daniele de Volterra, a former pupil of Michelangelo, was commissioned to undertake the task and thereafter became known as 'The Breeches Maker'.

SIX-TEN

In the argot of CB radio, 'six-ten' means to make love.

LEONARD SMITHERS

Smithers was an English publisher who got his sexual kicks from deflowering virgins, an obsession that gave rise to Oscar Wilde's celebrated remark that 'Smithers loves first editions'.

SPECIAL DELIVERY

Joseph Berkas, an Austrian philatelist who got into a spot of bother with the police following a misunderstanding at his digs, was given an absolute discharge when his case went before a court in Vienna. Asked to explain why he had burst into the bedroom of his landlady's attractive teenage daughter, torn away the towel with which she was drying herself and started a close fingertip search of her backside, Berkas explained that he had left a valuable foreign stamp soaking in the bath and returned to find that it had disappeared.

SPERM COUNT I
Faced with medical evidence that the number of Frenchmen
with below-average sperm counts had increased from twenty-
nine per cent to just over seventy per cent, a specialist laid the
blame on depression, anxiety, overwork, the use of tranquillizers
and insomnia.

SPERM COUNT II
The average man's ejaculate contains an estimated 200,000,000
sperm, although this represents just two per cent of the total
ejaculate; the other ninety-eight per cent consists of the mucus-
like semen.

SPIDER
The male spider's penis is found on the end of one of its legs.

SPINACH
Spinach, Popeye's favoured vegetable, is rich in iron and correspondingly ranks high in stimulating those parts that other
vegetables fail to reach.

SQUEEZE CONTROL
This was advocated by the pioneer sexologists Masters and
Johnson, as a satisfactory method for dealing with the common
problem of premature ejaculation. The technique involves the
woman masturbating her partner to the point where he cannot
control his ejaculation, whereupon she squeezes the tip of his
penis firmly between her fingers until the urge subsides. This is
repeated four or five times in each session. Once this technique
is mastered, the couple move to an intercourse position with
the woman on top. They remain like this motionless with the

woman stemming any premature ejaculatory urges by squeeze control, if the need arises. Later they move to a lateral position, with the woman applying squeeze control when required. Six months to a year of squeeze control leads to intercourse no more frequently than once a week, increasing as the problem subsides.

STRIP-TEASE

History was made in Paris on the night of 9 February 1893. That was the night of the Four Arts Ball held at the Moulin Rouge at which an artist's model by the name of Mona removed her clothes for the entertainment of the students present. This act of selfless good nature earned her a fine of one hundred francs and caused a riot in the Latin Quarter when enraged fans besieged the Prefecture of Police.

Just over a year later the world's first theatrical striptease was staged at a Parisian music hall under the title 'Le Coucher d'Yvette'. This showed a girl removing her clothes in preparation for going to bed. Other acts quick to cash in on the latest sensation showed equally becoming maidens shedding their clothes prior to bathing, being examined by a doctor, or sun bathing. Among the more imaginative was the one simply entitled 'La Puce' (The Flea) in which a young lady was obliged to strip herself garment by garment as she systematically searched for her unwelcome insect companion.

SUMO WRESTLING

It is quite usual for the powerful cremaster muscle to pull the testicles upwards and inwards when the outside temperature is cold. In extreme cases testicles can pop inside the inguinal canal in the groin and not be palpable in the scrotum at all.

This is a natural protective mechanism well understood by

Sumo wrestlers, who massage their testicles out of harm's way prior to getting to grips with an opponent.

SUNBATHING
Sixty years ago Lowestoft appointed an inspector of sunbathing.

ALGERNON SWINBURNE
The Victorian poet Algernon Swinburne lived a tortured sex life, heavily influenced by the beatings he received at Eton (where it was said the boys were required to sprinkle eau de cologne on themselves before the canings began). His principal sexual enjoyment seemed to come from sleeping with young boys and his one foray into a heterosexual relationship ended dismally with his middle-aged paramour complaining, 'I can't seem to make him understand that biting's no good.'

TESTICLE
The word 'testicle' has its roots in the Latin word for a 'witness'. In ancient Rome only witnesses with both testicles in place were allowed to give evidence in court.

TESTICLES
There is wide variation in the size of men's testicles, but on average they measure two inches long, an inch across and one-and-a-quarter inches in width.

Testicles start life in an unborn baby somewhere near the kidneys and descend into the scrotum (ball bag) at birth. The reason for this is that sperm production takes place at a temperature a couple of degrees lower than body temperature, so the process has to take place outside the body to function properly.

Thinking Makes It So

Researchers have identified four principal areas of sexual fantasies experienced by both men and women. Intimate fantasies include activities like making love with someone you love, or at least know; enjoying alfresco sex; oral sex; or being masturbated by a favourite partner. Then there are the more daring exploratory fantasies that dwell on ideas such as orgies; homosexual encounters; mixed race sex; and being seduced. Further from direct sexual experience are impersonal fantasies like watching others making love, stimulation by pornography and items like dildoes, leather and rubber wear. The fourth fantasy group indulges in sado-masochism.

To Be Or Not To Be

The State of Nevada is famous for the speed with which couples can marry – and divorce. So, when a couple named Holt decided to bring their marriage to an end, Mr Holt took himself off to Reno and filed a divorce suit. Three days later Mrs Holt arrived in town, and they spent the next three days together before she left. That, thought Mr Holt, was that – but Mrs Holt had other ideas and some time later applied through the courts for alimony. Her husband countered this on the grounds of the divorce he had been granted in Reno. This was met with a reply of condonation, that's to say his behaviour in Reno had demonstrated that he had forgiven his wife whatever actions on her part had forced him to seek a divorce in the first place. Mr Holt appealed and the case went before Judge Hitz, who found in favour of Mrs Holt and against her husband. 'Though we have seen much of the liberality of Nevada practice,' he told them, 'we assume that even in that forward-looking jurisdiction, parties to a case of divorce may not litigate by day and copulate by night.'

TOULOUSE-LAUTREC
In addition to being a hunchback the painter Toulouse-Lautrec suffered from a condition which endowed him with an over-sized penis. The two complaints combined to earn him the nickname 'teapot' among the girls in the brothel where he lived.

TRACK AND FIELD
In contrast to the commonly held belief that sex spoils athletic performance, Dr Craig Sharp, who used to act as medical adviser to British Olympic competitors, suggested that sexual activity might actually improve things. One Olympic athlete broke a world record only an hour after intercourse and a British athlete ran a four-minute mile just ninety minutes after getting down to it.

TRAILBLAZING
Some prostitutes in ancient Greece hit on a novel way of plying their trade. They took to wearing sandals with the words 'follow me' in Greek cut into the soles in mirror writing. When they walked along the streets wearing these, they left a trail of 'come-ons' that would-be clients could follow to their rooms.

TRICKS OF THE TRADE
According to one study of Scandinavian sex fairs, a popular sideshow was a form of sexual billiards in which participants tested their skill with marbles, and the vagina served as a pocket. 'The ladies will lift up their skirts,' runs the report, 'they will sit against the wall, their legs spread well apart. The gentlemen will take their places on the opposite side of the room ... Everyone has a try. The object is flick the glass marbles into the hole of this delightful billiard table. One can guess at the winner's reward.'

TRIKINI

The world first caught sight of a *bikini* on 5 July 1946, at a
fashion show in Paris — where else. Paraded down the cat-
walk by a dancer named Micheline Bernardi this new swimsuit
designed by Louis Réard took the world's breath away. Four
days earlier the USA had detonated an atomic bomb at Bikini
Atoll in the Pacific. The two events seemed related in their
headline impact and Mr Réard's creation was duly christened.
Mlle Bernardi wasn't forgotten in the excitement; she received
a reported 50,000 fan letters.

For nearly three decades the bikini reigned supreme. Then
New York, the rising fashion Mecca of the 1970s, offered the
world of swimwear the *trikini* in 1973. Billed as 'a new concept
designed to add new dimensions of poise', the trikini consisted
of a couple of pasties and pair of briefs. 'Most important,' ran
the press release, 'the cups cover the bosoms fully and stay on
in the water' — most important.

An enthusiastic crowd gathered for a poolside launching. In
dived the model wearing the new outfit. But when she broke
surface it became evident that she had mislaid two thirds of her
costume. What had started as tri was now uncompromisingly
mono — the bikini slept easily once more.

TROUSSEAU

As part of its policy of helping newly-weds, one department
store produced a list entitled 'Clothes for Your Honeymoon' to
assist young brides in choosing their all-important wardrobe.
Among the items listed was: 'Silk and lace nightdress (in case)'.

TURN-OFFS

The same American report into male sexuality that revealed
which stimuli men found most 'exciting' also reported that the
following turned them off the most:

1 Heavy make-up   80%
2 Leg or underarm hair   70%
3 Pregnancy   50%
4 Menstruation   42%

Turtle Dove

The seventeenth-century playwright Samuel Rowlands thought that powdered turtle dove would make a good aphrodisiac:

> Take me a turtle-dove
> And in an oven let her lie and bake
> So dry that you may powder of her make;
> Which, being put into a cup of wine,
> The wench that drink'st it will to love incline.

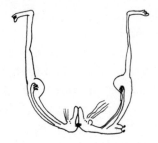

UNEMPLOYED: SHAKING HANDS WITH

There are dozens of euphemisms for masturbation, but in the course of her research into the subject Karen Shanor interviewed several hundred sexually active American men and came up with a list of the top ten most common masturbatory fantasies among men:

1 A nude or semi-nude female body (no mention, though, of whether the body is a familiar one or not).
2 Sex with a woman with whom the fantasizer had previously been involved.
3 A replay of a satisfying sexual experience.
4 Sex with two or more women.
5 Being considered a stud.
6 Watching a woman perform sex in an enticing way.
7 Clandestine sex.
8 Watching wife or lover having sexual relations with someone else.
9 Sex with a much younger woman.
10 Sex with somebody other than present lover.

Unexpected Visitors

While staying at The Vyne in Hampshire at the end of the last century, Lord Charles Beresford made a spectacular conquest which led to the object of his desire suggesting that they furthered their acquaintance in her room after the rest of the party had retired. Leaving her amour with strict instructions on how to find her, she retired to bed and waited.

Some time later, when the house had settled down to sleep, Lord Charles tiptoed out of his room and slipped along the corridors to his lady's chamber. When he found the door, he pulled off his dressing-gown and pyjamas, turned the handle, slipped inside and dived rapturously for the recumbent figure beneath the bedclothes. It soon became clear that somewhere in his furtive passage he had lost his way – that at least was the opinion expressed by the Bishop of Chester as he fended off Lord Charles's passionate advances.

Unlawful Sex

Faced with growing sexual liberation in the swinging sixties and permissive seventies, the House in Harrisburg, Pennsylvania voted by 180 to 69 to outlaw pre-marital and extra-marital sex in the state.

Unusual Side Effects of the Pill

It's generally accepted that oral contraceptives may slightly enlarge a woman's breasts, but in a few exceptional cases it has had other more alarming side-effects. Medical reports exist that show a woman being taken off the pill by her doctor after complaining of a rattling in her chest whenever she coughed. The doctor found that her breastbone was loose. Another patient developed loose teeth after going on the pill. In 1968 the *British Medical Journal* documented a case that suggested the pill might have been responsible for causing something akin to St Vitus's Dance.

Up for Sale
It's little more than a century ago that women were still being led to market to be sold to the highest bidder – in England. Prices ranged from five to twenty guineas, plus half a pint of beer, to a penny and a dinner.

Uppermost Limits
A decade ago the *Journal of Urology* carried an article which included the observation that, 'Prolonged intercourse, particularly with the female subject in the superior position, and inadvertent flexion of the erect penis are well-described cases of penile trauma commonly leading to corporeal rupture.'

Upwardly Mobile
In the course of his research Alfred Kinsey noticed that among many mammals the speed of erection was swift to say the least. Three to four seconds catered for most species, with others clocking considerably faster times. 'Stallions, bulls, rams, rats, guinea pigs, porcupines, cats, dogs, apes, and males of other species may come to full erection almost instantaneously upon contact with a sexual object,' reported Kinsey.

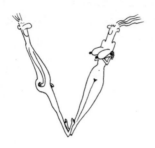

Vaginas: Two into one

Amazing as it sounds it is possible for a woman to have more than one vagina. The urogenital system is one of the common areas of the body to be affected by congenital, structural abnormality. Very often the vagina and part of the uterus can be separated into two parts by a fibrous partition and this may only come to light after difficulty when intercourse first takes place, or sometimes at the onset of pregnancy.

Valentine Messages

The author of *Poor Robin's Almanac* of 1729 dished out all sorts of advice to readers. Lonely hearts had this to look forward to in February:

> This month is propitious to lovers. And because many foolish things have been wrote by pretenders to astrology, relating to love and speedy marriage, I shall mention one sign only, which is infallible. In the evening of Valentine's Day, do take two white oak leaves, and lay them across your pillow, when you go to bed, putting on a clean shift

or shirt, and turning it the wrong side outwards, lay down and say these words aloud, 'Good Valentine be kind to me, in dreams let me my true love see.' So carefully drawing your right leg behind you, put it over your left shoulder. In like manner put your left leg behind you, laying it across your right shoulder; and be sure to take care that the soles of your feet meet under your chin. Then go to sleep as soon as you can. And if you dream you see two moons touching each other, you will certainly be marry'd very speedily, whether you be a young man, maid or widow.

Vehicle Registration

Back in 1973 cars in New York started displaying their new golden licence plates with three numbers and three letters in blue. Designed to replace the old blue plates with their yellow numbers, the State's Department of Motor Vehicles was proud of the fact that the new plates 'offer an almost infinite number of combinations', but was nervous about where some of those combinations might lead them. The department was 'determined to avoid sequences of letters that are obscene or insulting', and so put a complete ban on WET and DRY, on PIG and RAT, on FAG and DYK, on FEM and GYP, on ODD and POT, as well of course on SEX and SIN.

Velocity: ejaculation

The speed at which ejaculate is estimated to spurt from the penis says a lot about the pressure that's built up before its release. Tests show that it shoots out at only slightly less than the UK speed limit in built-up areas — namely twenty-eight miles an hour. Once in the vagina it's a different story, with the progress of the sperm reined in to an average speed of two feet every twenty-four hours.

VIBRATORS

Sex researchers in Sweden have concluded that the optimum speed for a satisfactory vibrator is sixty cycles per second. They also found that most women find greatest satisfaction from employing vibrators to the outer extremities of the vulva, rather than in deeper penetration.

VIEWING FIGURES

Researchers studying how various sexual acts on film aroused mixed audiences found:

1 Heterosexual sex – turned on men and women combined more than any other sexual activity shown.
2 Group sex – turned on men more than anything else, but was less of a turn-on for women.
3 Homosexual scenes – men were aroused more by watching two women making love than women were at watching two men. However, the sight of two women making love was less of a turn-off for women viewers than the sight of two men making love was for male viewers.
4 Heterosexual oral sex – both sexes were aroused, but women were more aroused than men.
5 Sado-masochistic sex – low turn-on for both sexes.
6 Masturbation – men were more turned-on watching women masturbate than women were watching men doing it. But women were less offended by the sight of a woman masturbating than men were at the sight of a man masturbating.

VIRGINITY: CAN IT BE RESTORED?
In theory the answer is yes! Although the importance of the hymen may have dwindled in western society, in the Middle East and Japan it still carries tremendous significance. Even today surgeons turn over a large number of patients for hymen replacements or repairs carried out in the strictest confidence and secrecy.

VIRGINITY: HOW TEN SHOW CELEBRITIES LOST THEIRS
1 Mick Jagger, aged sixteen, in a garden shed.
2 Mae West, aged thirteen, to her music teacher.
3 David Niven, aged fourteen, with a Soho prostitute named Nessie.
4 Art Buchwald, aged fifteen, to a hotel chambermaid.
5 Jerry Hall, aged fifteen, in a hayloft.
6 Ursula Andress, aged sixteen, in a photographer's studio.
7 Shirley MacLaine, aged sixteen, when drunk at a television producer's party.
8 Dyan Cannon, aged seventeen, to a choirboy.
9 Victoria Principal, aged eighteen, in the back of a Chevrolet.
10 Debbie Reynolds, aged twenty-three, to Eddie Fisher following their marriage.

VOTE RIGGING
When elections were held in Maine to elect the state's senators in 1978, Hayes E Gahagan stood for office on a strong right-wing, no nonsense ticket: abortion, women's rights and similarly liberal measures found little sympathy in his campaign. 'The vote I'm after is the Christian patriot', he avowed.

So intent was he in this quest that he, and one presumes the rest of his campaign staff, failed to notice the apparent contradictions in his official campaign photograph. Under closer examination a picture of a vagina was unmistakably blended with his hair, while the word 'SEX' nestled in the shadow of his right eye and beneath the knuckles of his left hand. The good people of Maine opted for another candidate.

WELFARE STATE
Seven recent reasons for requesting welfare payments:

1. Since I made an arrangement with the man in your office I am having a baby and my doctor says I should be getting more of it.
2. My husband got his project cut off two weeks ago, and I haven't had any relief since.
3. I cannot get sick pay. I have six children. Can you tell me why?
4. Please send me a form for having babies at reduced prices.
5. I have heard there are more than two ways you can have it and it works out cheaper the more you get if you have it the other way.
6. This is my eighth child. What are you going to do about it.
7. Unless my husband gets money pretty soon I will be forced to lead an immortal life.

Whales

As one might expect, the largest mammals are equipped with the largest reproductive organs. Whales' penises can reach a length of ten feet and in Blue Whales, the largest animals ever known to have existed, each testicle can measure over thirty inches and weigh up to one hundred pounds!

What's in a Name?

Ivor Krutch used to drive a taxi in Toronto. Violet Organ was a biographer and art historian. Private Parts once served in the US army. Mustafa Kunt served as a Turkish military attaché in Moscow. Oral Love managed a nursing home. Hyman Pleasure was Assistant Commissioner at the New York State Department of Mental Hygiene. And in 1963 *The Times* carried the cheerful news that a Mr Cock had married a Miss Prick.

Wheatgerm

This is one of the richest and most easily found sources of vitamin E, sometimes called 'the fertility vitamin'. Scientific work into the effects of vitamin E deficiency revealed that, in extreme cases, male animals deprived of the vitamin for a long period suffered irreparable damage to their testes. Further research showed that problems with conception and miscarriages were more frequent among societies where low levels of wheatgerm were consumed.

Whipping Boys

Towards the end of the eighteenth century began the vogue for flagellation, which was to run well into the following century. No whore house madam worthy of the name failed to offer this service, but Queen of them all was Mrs Theresa Berkley whose establishment in Charlotte Street was by far the best equipped of all. Recording some of the 'technical' details in her memoirs she listed, 'shafts with a dozen whip thongs in them; a dozen different sizes of cat-o'-nine-tails, some with needle-points worked into them; various kinds of thin bending canes; leather straps like coach traces; battledores, made of thick sole-leather with inch nails run through, and curry-combs.'

In addition to these she also kept a ready supply of scourges 'with which she often restored the dead to life': 'holly brushes, furze brushes; a prickly evergreen called butcher's bush' – and to give a refreshing taste of summer, green nettles!

WHOOPS!

A dozen dirty passages from the classics that say more than they mean:

> '... in winter his private balls were numerous enough for any young lady who was not suffering under the insatiable appetite of fifteen.' *Sense and Sensibility*, Jane Austen

> 'Mrs Goddard was the mistress of a School – not of a seminary, or an establishment, or any thing which professed, in long sentences of refined nonsense, to combine liberal acquirements with elegant morality upon new principles and new systems – and where young ladies for enormous pay might be screwed out of health and into vanity ...' *Emma*, Jane Austen

> 'A man who exposes himself when he is intoxicated, has not the art of getting drunk.' *Life of Samuel Johnson*, James Boswell

> 'He flourished his tool. The end of the lash just touched her forehead. A warm excited thrill ran through my veins, my blood seemed to give a bound, and then raced fast and hot along its channels. I got up nimbly, came round to

where he stood, and faced him.' *The Professor*, Charlotte
Brontë

'You brush it, till I grow aware,
　　Who wants me, and wide ope I burst.' *In a Gondola*,
Robert Browning

'She touched his organ, and from that bright epoch, even
it, the old companion of his happiest hours, incapable as
he had thought of elevation, began a new and deified
existence.' *Martin Chuzzlewit*, Charles Dickens

'Mrs Glegg had doubtless the glossiest and crispest curls
in her drawers, as well as curls in various degrees of fuzzy
laxness.' *The Mill on the Floss*, George Eliot

'Mr Longdon, resisting, kept erect with a low gasp that
his host only was near enough to catch. This suddenly
appeared to confirm an impression gathered by Van-
derbank in their contact, a strange sense that his visitor
was so agitated as to be trembling in every limb. It brought
to his lips a kind of ejaculation.' *The Awkward Age*, Henry
James

'The only thing I can think about now is being hard up. I
suppose having my hands in my pockets has made me
think about this. I always do sit with my hands in my
pockets, except when I am in the company of my sisters,
my cousins, or my aunts; and they kick up such a shindy –
I should say expostulate so eloquently on the subject –
that I have to give up and take them out – my hands I
mean.' *Idle Thoughts of an Idle Fellow*, Jerome K Jerome

'Well now, you look here, that was a good lay of yours
last night. I don't deny it was a good lay. Some of you
are pretty handy with a hand-spike end.' *Treasure Island*,
Robert Louis Stevenson

'All my heart
    Went forth to embrace him coming ere he came.' *Oenone*,
Alfred Lord Tennyson

'She gave a little scream and a jerk, and so relieved
herself ...' *The Duke's Children*, Anthony Trollope

Wig Club

Among the clubs frequented by the gentry of London in the
eighteenth century was the Wig Club which owed its name to
a wig, reputedly made of the pubic hair of the mistresses of
King Charles II. Any gentleman intending to join was required
to produce a lock of his own mistress's pubic hair to be woven
in with the original.

Oscar Wilde

Wilde's brother, William, said of him, 'Oscar is a perfect gentleman. You can trust him with a lady anywhere.' While the lady
who doubtlessly trusted him most, his wife, said sadly, 'I think
his fate is rather like Humpty Dumpty's, quite as tragic and
quite as impossible to put right'.

Others were less charitable. Algernon Swinburne (whose own
private life didn't bear much close scrutiny) wrote the cruel
epitaph for Wilde:

> When Oscar came to join his God
> Not earth to earth but sod to sod,
> It was for sinners such as this
> Hell was created bottomless.

After his release from prison, Wilde went to spend his final few
years in France. There he was persuaded by a friend to visit a
brothel in Dieppe, from which he emerged with the verdict,
'The first these ten years, and it will be the last. It was like cold

mutton. But tell it in England, for it will entirely restore my character.'

WILLPOWER ALONE
Of the 5,000 men that were surveyed in the course of the Kinsey research, no more than four (0.08 per cent of the survey) were found who could reach ejaculation by fantasy alone, without the aid of manual or other stimulation.

THE WILMINGTON GIANT
The Wilmington Giant is one of the most impressive chalk figures in the British Isles. Measuring over 200 feet from head to toe it stands proudly on the south of Windover Hill, a few miles inland from Eastbourne. In spite of the figure's obvious archaeological and anthropological interest, there is no denying its anatomical prowess, as one correspondent to the local paper made clear.

'For many years I have wished to ask my aunt to visit our beautiful town,' she wrote, 'but have been deterred from doing so by the knowledge that she would have to pass this stark, staring figure.

'Surely it would be possible to fit this disgusting effigy with some kind of hessian kilt; or, failing this, perhaps a strategically planted row of shrubbery might serve.'

WOMEN'S CRICKET
Before the Second World War it was still decreed by the Women's Cricket Association that women cricketers should wear white stockings – a rule which it has to be said was not always adhered to by the players.

WRITING

The French novelist Honoré de Balzac was convinced that the quality of his writing was directly related to the amount of sperm he retained in his body. Sex the night before picking up his pen apparently impaired his literary powers. On one occasion he suffered an uncontrollable 'outburst' during his sleep and reckoned it cost him a masterpiece the next morning.

X-CERTIFICATE FILM
The first film to be given an X-certificate (for viewing by adults only) was the French film *La Vie Commence Demain* (*Life Begins Tomorrow*) which opened in the UK on 9 January 1951. It earned its rating and its place in cinema history because of a sequence that dealt with artificial insemination.

XMAS GREETINGS
The messages on Christmas cards usually follow fairly predictable lines, which made the one discovered by a little girl on a card sent to her granny in Tyne and Wear all the more remarkable. Asking granny what it meant, the child read aloud the jingle:

> A robin redbreast on my sill
> Sang for a crust of bread
> I slowly brought the window down
> And smashed its fucking head.

Granny wrote to the Greeting Card Association asking, not unreasonably, whether this was really the sort of message to convey the essential meaning of Christmas. After the festive season she received a reply to the effect that the verse was some 120 years old and was well known to card collectors.

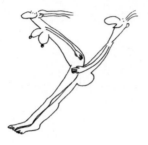

A YARD OF FILM

That was the ruling that film censors once imposed on film producers who showed a kiss on the screen. One yard of film amounted to thirty-six seconds of snogging and early movie stars like Rudolph Valentino milked them for all they were worth.

YOUNG AT HEART

In 1984 the BBC Schools Broadcasting Unit celebrated its Diamond Jubilee by repeating one of its golden moments. This was a music and movement class for a bygone age in which the woman teacher was encouraging her young listeners to have fun with their balls:

> We are going to play a hiding and finding game. Now, are your balls high up or low down? Close your eyes a minute and dance around, and look for them. Are they high up? Or are they low down? If you have found your balls, toss them over your shoulder and play with them.

Youngest Ejaculator
Sexual researchers have found several cases of boys as young as eight experiencing full scale ejaculation. In one less reliably authenticated case the boy was only six at the time!

You're In The Army Now
This was the 1941 film in which Jane Wyman (the first Mrs Ronald Reagan) set a record for a kiss on screen, when she and Regis Toomey held a three-minute clinch while the cameras rolled (actually they kept it going for 185 seconds – but who's counting?).

You Said It
Twenty quotes that lay it on the line:

1 'I have often thought that I would like to be a saddle on a bike' – W H Auden

2 'I hate the whole sex scene. I put a bottle over the head of anybody who tries to chat me up.' – Toyah Wilcox

3 'If I were to come back in another life, I would like to be Warren Beatty's finger-tips.' – Woody Allen

4 'Men are like naughty little boys, they want the bar of candy they can't have. When they've got it at home they go out and look for another piece.' – Jackie Collins

5 'Love is two minutes fifty-two seconds of squishing sounds.' – Johnny Rotten

6 'I used to be Snow White but I drifted.' – Mae West

7 'A man is only as old as the women he feels.' – Groucho Marx

8 'Men are those creatures with two legs and eight hands.' – Jayne Mansfield

9 'Women are a problem, but if you haven't already guessed, they are the kind of problem I enjoy wrestling with.' – Warren Beatty.

10 'Bigamy is having one husband too many. Monogamy is the same.' – Erica Jong

11 'Whoever named it necking was a poor judge of anatomy.' – Groucho Marx

12 'Sex appeal is fifty per cent what you've got and fifty per cent what people think you've got.' – Sophia Loren

13 'If I jumped on all the dames I am supposed to have jumped on I would never have had time to go fishing.' – Clark Gable

14 'Before you meet your handsome prince you have to kiss a lot of toads. Macho doesn't mean mucho.' – Zsa Zsa Gabor

15 'I think pop music has done more for oral intercourse than anything else that ever happened and vice versa.' – Frank Zappa

16 'Nature abhors a virgin – a frozen asset.' – Clare Boothe Luce

17 'Sex – the poor man's polo.' – Clifford Odets

18 'Husbands are chiefly good lovers when they are betraying their wives.' – Marilyn Monroe

19 'The good thing about masturbation is that you don't have to dress up for it.' – Truman Capote

20 'I thought *coq au vin* was love in a lorry.' – Victoria Wood

ZINGUA, QUEEN OF ANGOLA

Early in the seventeenth century this formidable lady held sway over Angola and conducted a bizarre and brutal sex life with what seems like most of its male population. Her royal palace was stabled with a large harem of lovers whom she would periodically parade for battles to the death in order to sleep with the victors. Not that she showed undue favouritism. After sleeping with a man all night it was not uncommon for her to have him executed the next morning. Out of jealousy she had all pregnant women executed as well. According to early missionary records Queen Zingua continued this remarkable sex life until the age of seventy-seven when she was converted to Roman Catholicism – in the nick of time.

Famous Last Words

Five enduring epitaphs:

1
                    BRIGHAM YOUNG
                Born on this spot 1801
                 A man of courage
              and superb equipment

2
   Here lies (the Lord have mercy on her!)
   One of Her Majesty's maids of honour:
     She was young, slender and pretty;
    She died a maid – the more the pity

3
        Here lies poor Charlotte
         Who died no harlot,
         But in her virginity;
         Of the age nineteen,
          In this vicinity,
       Rare to be found or seen

4
     Here lies the body of Martha Dias
  Who was always uneasy, and not overpious;
  She lived to the age of three score and ten,
And gave to the worms what she refused to men

5
  Here lie two poor lovers, who had the mishap
   Tho' very chaste people, to die of the clap.
    [They were killed by lightning.]

Sex

For those who didn't manage to match the words and their definitions on pages 136–7, here are those twenty-four words and their correct definitions:

Sextuple – six-fold.

Sexavalent – having a chemical valency of six.

Sexfid – divided into six segments.

Sextoncy – the office of a sexton.

Sexennium – a period of six years.

Sexannarian – a six-year-old child.

Sextans – a bronze coin of the Roman Republic.

Sexen – a long fishing boat propelled by six oars.

Sexvirate – a body of six colleagues.

Sexfoil – having six leaves.

Sexagene – multiplied by sixty or a power of sixty.

Sexto – a piece of paper cut six to a sheet.

Sexdigital – having six fingers.

Sextipartition – divisions into sixths.

Sexagenary – based on the number sixty.

Sexagecuple – proceeding by sixties.

Sexious – sectarian.

Sexcuple – to multiply by six.

Sexadecimal – relating to sixteen.

Sexennial – occurring every six years.

Sexdigit – person with six fingers.
Sexmillennary – of six thousand years.
Sextain – stanza of six lines.
Sextile – measured by sixty degrees.